Invicta

A Biography of R.C.M. Jenkins

By
Mark Rothwell

With Contributions from Brian P. Jenkins & Robert D. Mott

First published in 2017 by CreateSpace Independent Publishing Platform. © Mark Rothwell

All rights reserved. No part of this book may be reproduced or transmitted in any form or by any means, electronic or mechanical, including photocopying, recording or by any information storage or retrieval system without written permission from the copyright holder.

Design, Layout & Typeset by: - Mark Rothwell
Front cover image: - 'R.C.M. Jenkins' courtesy Brian P. Jenkins
Edited by: - Brian P. Jenkins & Robert D. Mott

ISBN 13: 978-1548270063 - ISBN 10: 1548270067

Also by Mark Rothwell

Policing the West Country (Published 2017)

Acknowledgements

Katie Herbert, Jill Drysdale, Carmen Talbot, Anna Derham, Holly Wells, Rev. Alan Pinnegar, Roger Hext, Heather Mott, Simon Dell, Ken Searle, Sean Hollands, Rosemary Hollands, Neil Woods, Peter Ferris, Roy Ingleton and Hilary Bracegirdle.

Special Thanks To

Kristina L. Evans, Brian P. Jenkins, Paul R. Jenkins, Peter B. Jenkins, Tina Machado and Robert D. Mott.

Dedication

Robert Cyril Morton Jenkins O.B.E., K.P.M., O St. J. A stalwart son of Kent, farmhand, soldier, policeman, chief constable, businessman, sportsman, husband, father and grandfather.

Contents

Farmhand to Footslogger	……………………..5
Corfe's Irregulars	……………………..29
Policing the Cathedral City	……………………..35
West to the Holy Headland	……………………..48
Scandal in Hellfire Corner	……………………..75
A Force for the County	……………………..80
The Growing of the Apple	……………………..96
Remembering Uncle Cyril	……………………..110
Some Reminiscences	……………………..113
Author's Note	……………………..132
Acknowledgements	……………………..135

Farmhand to Footslogger

Robert Cyril Morton Jenkins, 'Cyril' to his loved ones and 'Jenks' to his friends, grew up in a time when every man, woman and child 'knew their place.' People worked where they were raised and came to respect the town and townspeople as their ancestors had. It was a class-conscious society divided by the educated rich, uneducated poor and somewhere in between the skilled working-class who afforded education depending on their circumstances.

The Jenkins family, farmers in the Stalisfield area of Faversham in Kent, were hard-working folk with a modest income. William Jenkins, a woodcutter by trade, was able to send Cyril, whom he and his wife Bertha adopted in 1898, to school in Stalisfield Green and much of his formative years were spent hard at work on the orchards.

By his own admission, the juvenile Cyril was never a gifted farmer and was better suited to dealing with the family accounts. Whatever path in life he intended to take, everything changed with the outbreak of the First World War.

The war to end all wars

In the seventeen months from 7th August 1914, the Secretary of State for War Lord Kitchener led a far-reaching campaign to form infantry battalions from enlisted members without recourse for conscription. The renowned strapline 'Kitchener Wants You' was a powerful tool in his arsenal, and he left it to local councils to raise these 'Pals' battalions free from the interference of the War Office (once they were raised and trained however, the War Office absorbed them into the Army.)

Although one could take the clichéd view that Cyril followed Kitchener's pointed finger to the nearest enlistment centre, it is more likely he saw the call for volunteers in an edition of a local newspaper. It was a tactic employed by many of the battalions formed at Kitchener's behest, and the adverts were designed to appeal – promises of free cigarettes, comfortable billets and the opportunity to participate in sports were attractive propositions for young working-class men who otherwise lived just within their means. Indeed, not all those who enlisted were *men*, rather they were boys aged fourteen, fifteen or sixteen who flocked to the colours to play their part. Cyril was only sixteen years old – like so many others, he added two years to his age when he enlisted.

"The Queen's Own Royal West Kent Regiment

'The Regiment that never loses a trench.'

The 11th Bn. is in comfortable billets in Lewisham (within easy distance of London by train or by tram.) The Headquarters are on the Private Banks Ground. This is one of the finest Cricket Grounds in the South of England. Boxing, cricket, football, and all kinds of conceivable SPORT are encouraged and many excellent Smoking Concerts (cigarettes free) arranged for the amusement of the men.

COME AND BRING YOUR PALS

You can ENLIST together, PLAY together, TRAIN together

And FIGHT together.

Any further particulars can be obtained from Lieut. G.F. Pragnell, Private Banks Ground, Catford SE. Phone Lee Green 631."

Above. Call for men to enlist in the 11th (Lewisham) Battalion Queen's Own Royal West Kent Regiment. Kitchener's 'Pals' battalions were built from ordinary citizens volunteering without recourse for conscription.

It was a popular view that the war would be 'over by Christmas' yet when the campaign in Europe spiralled into an attrition war, conscription was introduced and many of the regiments yet to set foot in France and Belgium were reorganised and absorbed into others. Cyril enlisted and trained with the 2/1 Royal East Kent Yeomanry in 1914, spending the next two years learning how to use a rifle, taking instruction in drill and making bonds that would define him in later life. The regiment experienced significant change in the first two years of the war.

Originally a mounted regiment, in July 1916 it was converted to a cyclist unit in the 7th Cyclist Brigade, 2nd Cyclist Division and relocated from Canterbury to Manningtree, Essex. In November, the division was broken up and the 2/1 regiment was merged with the 2/1 Queen's Own West Kent Yeomanry to form the 9th (East and West Kent) Yeomanry Cyclist Regiment, 3rd Cyclist Brigade, based out of Ipswich.

Joining the 'Blind Half-Hundred'

Before the regiment relocated to Ipswich, Cyril was one of two-hundred-and-fifty yeomanry men sent to the front and absorbed with the 11th (Lewisham) Queen's Own Royal West Kent Regiment at a village in Northern France called Ribemont. The 11th was a Pals battalion raised by the Mayor of Lewisham in response to Kitchener's call for another 300,000 men. Beginning on 5th May 1915, the battalion trained at Catford and joined the 118th Brigade, 39th Division in July. In January 1916, the battalion relocated to Aldershot for final training and, in May 1916, sailed to France as part of the 123rd Brigade, 41st Division, under Major General Sydney Lawford. The 11th set foot in northern France on 3rd May 1916 and settled with the Division between Hazebrouck and Ballieul. By the time Cyril joined the 11th, the battalion had already suffered many casualties, including the loss of battalion leader Lieutenant Colonel A.F. Townsend on 15th September 1916 during the Battle of Flers-Courcelette.

Broomfield Hall, Herne Bay, September 1914. Cyril, sitting front-row-left, enlisted with the 2/1 Royal East Kent Yeomanry. *(Brian P. Jenkins)*

Broomfield Hall Stables, 1914. Cyril is stood to the left of the horse. *(Brian P. Jenkins)*

Broomfield Hall grounds, 1914. Larking about was an important part of battalion life! *(Brian P. Jenkins)*

Broomfield Hall, 21st March 1915. One of the many buildings requisitioned for use by the War Office for enlisted men to train. *(Brian P. Jenkins)*

The **'Hollies'**, **Herne, 1915.** Taken from Cyril's own photo album, these men are thought to be the Jordan brothers, Bertie, Frank and William. *(Brian P. Jenkins)*

Bridge Camp near Canterbury, 1916. Cyril is in the front row, second from left. *(Brian P. Jenkins)*

A battle of famous firsts

Flers-Courcelette was a battle of famous firsts, notably the pioneering use of tanks by the British Army in any conflict, but also because of the presence of New Zealand and Canadian troops on The Somme battlefield for the first time. The German Army, also making strides in technological warfare, unleashed the 'Albatros' D.I. fighter plane into the skies above The Somme. The British Mark I tanks – metal behemoths previously unseen on any battlefield – ambled slowly over the jagged and ruined remains of the villages of Flers and Courcelette. It seemed this new warfare would send the enemy running, but it was far from the case. 'Footsloggers' like Cyril Jenkins found they could easily march past the sluggish Mark I, which at around 28 tons could barely muster 4 miles per hour!

Mud-filled shell holes

'No man's land' was an appropriate expression, and it was here that Cyril saw many of the war's horrors. Artillery fire from 'ten-mile snipers'[1] left the battlefield pitted with mud-filled shell holes, and many wounded men drowned in them. Bodies that could not be rescued imminently were left for many days while both sides languished in a stalemate and the smell was horrifying. Men like Cyril had to find ways to remain positive and it was a welcome reprieve in the winter of 1916 that the trench-tired battalion was rotated away from the dugouts for Christmas. The camp at St. Eloi[2] was alive with festive cheer, although temperatures were at times freezing.

'Have you rubbed your feet today?'

The conditions faced by the 11th were dreadful and trench foot was a serious problem. The advice from the War Office was to apply whale oil to the feet and dry socks over a fire

---

[1] Allied artillery operators were colloquially known as 'ten-mile snipers' and were often responsible for devastating incidents of friendly fire.

[2] Such was the reprieve enjoyed, he later chose 'St. Eloi' as the name for his house at Whitstable Road, Canterbury, in the 1930s.

during respite. Colonel Corfe, successor to the late A.F. Townsend, made it his duty to ensure the battalion marched on well-oiled feet and during the daily round at Spoil Bank often asked, 'have you rubbed your feet today?' Such was Corfe's insistence on the practice that his expression found its way into one of the many 'ditties' sung by the battalion to the tune of 'Mademoiselle from Armentieres.'

The Colonel on his rounds today, parlez-vous?
The Colonel as he passed our way, parlez-vous?
The Colonel on his rounds one day, said 'Have you rubbed your feet today?'
Inky-pinky, parlez-vous?[i]

A runner's lot

Cyril's lot was an unenviable one. Battalion communications relied upon men known as 'runners' who ferried messages and rum between dugouts, often under heavy machine gun fire. As runner for 'D' Company, Cyril and fellow runner Bertie Jordan got into a sticky situation one evening in 1917.

"Late that night Jordan and I had to go up to the front line with messages and rum. We left Opal Reserve at the same spot as we had done earlier in the evening and tried to strike the front line, as before. We walked a long way and then struck some German

wire. I assumed that it was their old front line and got through. We went on a few yards when a German flare was sent up and we heard a German challenge. We lay low for some time and then made our way back through the wire, where we were at once challenged by one of our own patrols. It proved to be Corpl. S. Port, of 'D' Company, and his men, covering the R.E. wiring party in front of our line. We had been about 200 yards ahead of this. It was a case of 'where ignorance is bliss.' When we were brought in, the frontline people took us for a couple of prisoners and I well remember the astonishment and remarks of Mr. Malpass, as he recognised us. His remarks were, however, mild compared to my half section, Jordan, when he heard the German challenge and we realised where we were. 'A fine guide you are, etc, etc.'"

The battalion that never ran out of rum

Thanks to the chance encounter of an abandoned rum cart by the 'D' Company Quartermaster in 1916, the 11th became known as the 'battalion that never ran out of rum.' Soldiers filled their canteens with as much of the fine liquid as they could carry, ensuring jollity and warmth for the remainder of the war.

1916 Christmas card. Sent to all the men of the 41st Division. The card depicts a disgruntled German prisoner being led away by a British soldier. *(IWM)*

By the summer of 1917, the 11th was in the relative haven of Ploegsteert Wood in Belgium in anticipation for the attack on Messines Ridge. Previously a hotly contested battleground in the early days of the war, 'Plugstreet' was by this time a place for allied soldiers to find rest and recuperation.

'Our most successful attack'

The Battle of Messines was an attempt to remove the German Army's ability to attack merchant shipping in the English Channel by driving them out of the Belgian coast. General Sir Hubert Plumer, commander of the British Second Army, recommended to Field Marshall Sir Douglas Haig that the capture of Messines-Wytschaete Ridge, in Western Flanders, would achieve that objective. Planning for the attack was enormously complex and involved sophisticated use of aerial photography, field surveys, more detailed maps, weather data, sound-ranging equipment and flash spotting[3] to acquaint British artillery with German targets on the ground.

British tunnelling units from the Royal Engineers secretly planted mines under the German Fourth Army line near Mesen which were detonated at 0310 on 7th June 1917

---

[3] Observing the bearing of the muzzle flashes of enemy guns to provide intersections indicating the location of guns.

signalling the start of the battle. The explosion is regarded by historians as the most powerful seen on a battlefield at that point and left nineteen enormous craters. On the eve of the attack, General Plumer's chief of staff General Sir Charles Harrington remarked to the press 'Gentleman, we may not make history tomorrow, but we shall certainly change the geography.' Historians disagree over whether the battle was a success, although those on the ground certainly thought so, including Cyril who considered it 'our most successful attack.'

Dummy tree on Hill 63, 7th June 1917. The tree was used by the Australian Army as an observation post during the Battle of Messines 7th – 14th June 1917. *(Australian War Memorial)*

Ruined German trench following the Battle of Messines. The opening British mine attack killed over 10,000 German troops. *(National Library of Scotland)*

From July to September the 11th saw action at the Third Ypres in the battles at Hollebeke Village and Tower Hamlets, before enjoying another reprieve on the relatively temperate region of La Panne on the Belgian coast.

The 'show' as a runner saw it

An indication of how dangerous a runner's job was can be found in Cyril's own account of the Third Ypres after the capture of Hollebeke Village by the British. Driving rain had rendered the battlefield a sea of mud making any advance extremely challenging. Regardless, the British

Army conducted several offensives in the arena from 31st July – 10th November 1917 at great human cost.

'On the morning of the 31st I was at 'Bow'[4] when the offensive opened. We soon learned that things were not going too well up in front and a party from HQ, runners, snipers, batmen and signallers, etc., was sent up under Lieutenant R.G. Rogers. The mud and water was terrible, up to knees everywhere. Upon leaving our front line we followed a shallow German trench, the water in places being up to our waists, where shells had burst. Sniping was bad.

We reached a small bridge over trench, to go under which meant water up to our top tunic pockets. Two T.M.B.[5] men following us saw this and started to go over the top. One of them was at once hit by a sniper and we decided to go underneath. We reached a shallow trench, where we were ordered to consolidate. Hollebeke Church lay to our half right front and there was a small copse on our left. Several dead and wounded Germans were in the trench.

Towards mid-day we saw a German near the church repeatedly waving his overcoat in the air. Saw several targets in front but we had only our rifles which were choked with mud. A German plane worried us considerably, constantly swooping down and firing on us. Then a flight of our 'Triplanes' came over, the first I

---

[4] 'Bow' was the code name for battalion headquarters.
[5] T.M.B. – Trench Mortar Battalion

had seen. By dusk we had dug quite a respectable trench. Mr Rogers went off to the left to get into touch and Sergeant Haydon (Machine Gun Sergeant) went to the right.

As darkness fell, a party of Germans ran towards us. We at first thought it a counter-attack but found that they were unarmed and wished to give themselves up. Shelling of our trench then started, high velocity, 'rubber-heeled' stuff. It was very accurate, in front and behind, eventually coming right into trench. Corporal Nicholls of snipers was in charge and when shelling got too hot he ordered us to get back and line shell holes. Then we found in the darkness that some wire had been put up behind us. In scrambling through this, Witten fell on to it and got a barb into the side of his eye making a nasty wound. (Witten was my batman, and a fine fellow. One of the Yeoman, he was formerly a runner, always cheery and willing, brave to a fault. We had shared many exciting reconnaissance.) I was instructed to take him down to HQ and get some orders, for we seem to be isolated. There were about 12 in the party. On the way I found one of our gunners with shell shock, he was crying like a child.

I remember Witten was unnerved by his wound and by the time we reached Bow I was as bad, if not worse, than either. At Bow, the first person I saw was Sergeant Major Aldridge (certainly one of the most pleasant Sergeant Majors I ever met.) He was very surprised to see me as the word had gone round that the party had been captured. Apparently someone in touch with HQ had seen the party of Germans come over to us. I went in to see Colonel Corfe and, on his map, pointed out where I had been and where my party was. I was then given a tot of whiskey and given the Sergeant Major's bunk to sleep in. I next remember Mr Aldridge waking me (I had slept for 12 hours) and instructing me to go in and see Colonel Corfe.

From the Colonel I learned that Captains Lindsay and Rooney and Lieutenant Rogers were in Hollebeke, at a dugout where I had seen the German waving his coat. I was to find a pal and go up to him (Captain Lindsay) with rations and messages. I went upstairs and found a good fellow, 'Dasher' Wildash. We were given a good meal by Corporal Charlie Neave (he was a wonderful fellow, always a meal from somewhere and a tot of something in his water bottle) and then set off on our walk.

We went round the front of the copse I have mentioned and then turned right for Hollebeke Village. Snipers soon sent us to cover and then we had to cover the remaining distance by short rushes, doubling right and left from shell hole to shell hole. Arriving at Hollebeke we found the officers in a dugout, at cross roads opposite the church. The street lamp, a pre-war relic, was still lying outside the dugout. Two prisoners were in the dugout, one, the elder, was wounded; he was incessantly calling 'Yacob, Yacob' to the younger and it was some time before I tumbled to the fact that the younger one was named 'Jacob.' One drawback to the dugout was that it faced the German line and repeatedly a bullet would 'plop' against the opposite wall. We had to sit back close to the side walls to keep out of the line of fire.

There were about 30 men in the village and hardly any N.C.O.s. The officers had been on the go from daybreak of the 31st, it now being midday of the 1st. Wildash and I were instructed to stay. As evening came on we commenced to patrol from post to post, of which there were four, and so we carried on throughout the night. The only N.C.O. I remember was Lance Corporal Clift, who was constantly working on his Lewis Gun, which through a defect he could only fire as a rifle, one round at a time. All rifles were choked with mud, bombs were very scarce, and what was worse some of the men on one of the posts hardly knew the first thing about using them. They were from a new draft and had in their previous unit been employed on the transport.

We saw several Germans very close during the night but as they were not molesting us and we were in a most precarious state, we thought discretion the better part of valour. As day broke, Wildash and I went hunting around the dugouts for anything in the shape of souvenirs, but sniping again cramped our style.

We went down into one cellar, water still about knee-deep, and found a tunnel leading towards the enemy lines. We traversed this for some distance but could not find the end, eventually we turned about and immediately got the wind up, falling over each other in our hurry as though there were a hundred Jerries after us. I recall how disgusted we were with ourselves when we regained the surface and daylight. One thing we brought in was a little 'fish tail' gun. It was eventually taken down the line as a trophy.'[ii]

Early in 1918, the battalion was conveyed by train to the Mantua region of Italy as part of the Italian Expeditionary Force, taking the frontline near the River Piave, northwest of Treviso. They endured torrid conditions on this tour of duty, inhabiting vacated Italian trenches that were ankle-deep in human waste.

They remained in Italy for three months before returning to the Western Front in time for the German Spring Offensive. On 11th March 1918, seeing the end of the war in sight, the War Office decided to reduce the number of battalions in the Royal West Kent Regiment and on 16th March the 11th (Lewisham) Battalion was no more. Cyril was relocated to the 8th Battalion for the remainder of the war.

Back west and on to Armistice

From 8th August to 11th November 1918, the 41st Division launched offensives against the Central Powers, successfully pushing the Germans out of France in a series of battles that became known as the Hundred Days

Offensive. The Germans retreated beyond the Hindenburg Line and by war's end casualties for the 11th before disbandment totalled 1,812 out of a force of 3,000, and for the 41st Division 32,158 killed, wounded or missing. It was during this final push that Jenkins was wounded in the leg, cruelly robbing him of a commission.

Royal West Kent Regiment cap badge. The prancing horse is the symbol for the County of Kent and is traditionally white on a red background on the county flag. The Latin 'Invicta' translates simply to 'invincible' or 'unconquered' and is the motto of Kent. The regiment was founded in 1881 and was known by various monikers including *The Blind Half-Hundred, The Celestials, The Devil's Royals* and *The Dirty Half-Hundred*. (British Military Badges)

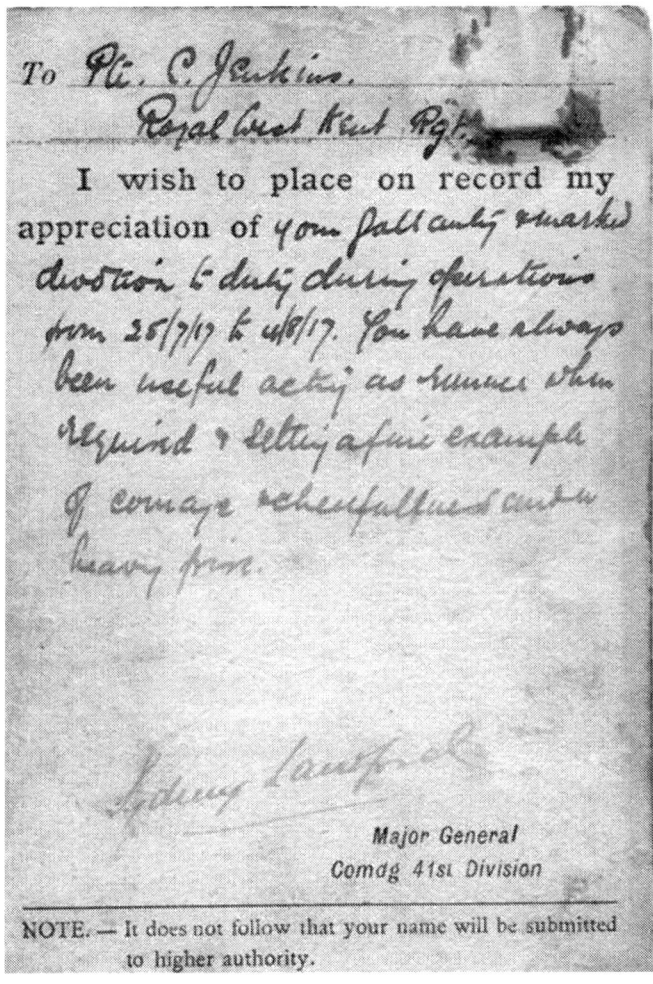

The note reads: "I wish to place on record my appreciation of your gallant and marked devotion to duty during operations from 25/7/17 to 4/8/17. You have always been useful acting as runner when required and setting a fine example of courage and cheerfulness under heavy fire." *(Brian P. Jenkins)*

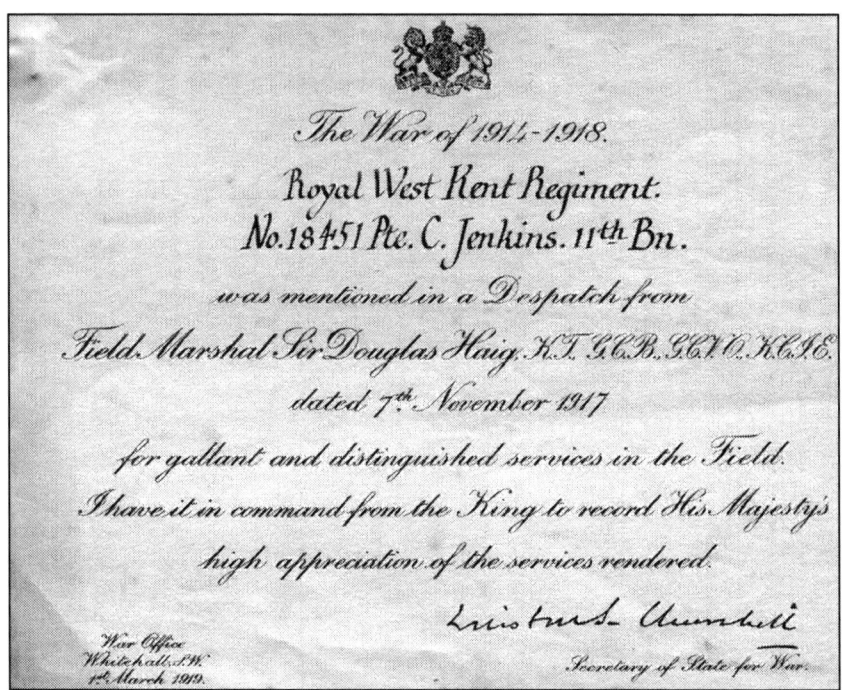

Mentioned in Dispatches. One of the greatest honours was to be 'Mentioned in Dispatches' by the Secretary of State for War. Soldiers who performed gallant or meritorious actions in the face of the enemy were noted in official reports which were then referred to high command. The Secretary of State for War, who succeeded Lord Kitchener upon his death in 1916, was Winston Churchill. *(Brian P. Jenkins)*

The 11th (Lewisham) Battalion 'Corfe's Irregulars'

Summary

5th May 1915 – raised at Lewisham by the Mayor and a local committee, trained at Catford. Joined the 118th Brigade in 39th Division in July 1915. Moved to the 122nd Brigade in October 1915. Relocated to Aldershot in January 1916 and landed in France on 3rd May 1916. In November 1917 moved with the Division to Italy and returned to France, arriving at Doullens on 7th March 1918.

16th March 1918 – disbanded and merged with other battalions.

Commanding Officers

Lt. Col. H.L. Searle	5 May 1915 – Feb 1916
Lt. Col. A.F. Townsend	Feb 1916 – 15 Sept 1916 (KIA)
Lt. Col. A.C. Corfe (wounded)	15 Sept 1916 – 20 Sept 1917
Lt J.C. Beadle M.C.	20 Sept 1917 – 8 Jan 1918
Maj. A.J. Jiminez M.C.	8 Jan 1918 – 21 Feb 1918
Lt. Col. A.C. Corfe D.S.O.	21 Feb 1918 – 16 Mar 1918

Lt. Col. A.C. Corfe DSO, 1945. Twice leader of the 11th (Lewisham) Battalion, the inimitable Arthur Cecil Corfe (standing at microphone) was a New Zealand-born Australian rugby union player, and represented his country in the sport in 1899. He remained in the Army Reserves until 1933. *(Brian P. Jenkins)*

Notable Engagements
15-22 Sept 1916 – Battle of Flers-Courcelette
7-14 Jun 1917 – Battle of Messines
20-23 Sept 1917 – Battle of Tower Hamlets

Casualties
2,064 killed, missing or wounded, viz. 484 ORs and 23 Officers killed, 306 ORs and 1 Officer missing and 1,208 ORs and 42 Officers wounded.

They left as boys and returned as men. Thought to be pictured in 1919 with fellow company 'runner' Bertie Jordan, who perished under tragic circumstances in 1920 when he fell while working from Stone Pier, Stone, near Dartford. *(Brian P. Jenkins)*

Old Comrades Association

Thanks to the vociferous enthusiasm of former 'D' Company Quartermaster Sergeant L.W. Dawson, an 'Old Comrades Association' (O.C.A.) for the 11th Battalion was founded in 1932 and held its first meeting on 27th January of that year at Folkestone's Raglan Hotel. Over eighty ex-11th members were in attendance and, with tongue firmly in cheek, were much preoccupied with remarking how 'big and fat' each had become since 1919!

Dawson was inspired to form the association after hearing news that the 41st Division's memorial to the fallen, in the village of Flers, was erected in 1923 but not completed due to a lack of funds. The 11th Queen's Royal West Surrey Regiment O.C.A. was planning a pilgrimage to Flers and a Captain E.W.J. Neave penned an article for *Live Wire* magazine asking for anyone interested in attending and helping complete the memorial to get in touch. Dawson read the article and contacted Neave and the idea of an O.C.A. for 'Corfe's Irregulars' came to the fore. At the Raglan Hotel meet, Lt. Colonel Corfe D.S.O. was elected O.C.A. President in absentia (as he was in Athens at the time) with other senior battalion officers taking vice-president, chairman and treasury roles accordingly.

The first reunion dinner took place on 5th March 1932 at Slater's Restaurant in High Holborn, London, and featured a menu specially tailored for the 11th Battalion. Over 120 men, including Cyril, dined on delights such as Consommé *Flers*, Thick Ox Tail *La Messines* and *Ploegsteert Pudding*. Much drink was consumed and many departed well-oiled.

11th Battalion reunion, 1932. The 'Old Comrades Association' was founded in January 1932 by L.W. Dawson, formerly of 'D' Company, and held its first reunion dinner on 5th March at Slater's Restaurant, High Holborn, London. Cyril bottom left corner. (© *Military Archive*)

With old friendships rekindled, the 11th O.C.A. was on firm footing to conduct the pilgrimage to Flers and Cyril joined 350 comrades from the 41st Division on a tour of the old battlefields on Whitsun 1932. The hamlet they last saw as a pile of rubble was a bustling and happy community once again and joined them in unveiling the finished memorial.

Battlefield pilgrimage, c1932. Photographed near Bedford House Cemetery, Ypres. Cyril far right next to ruined wall. *(Brian P. Jenkins)*

11th Battalion Reunion, 1952. The 'Old Comrades Association' was an important touchstone for 11th Battalion veterans. Cyril foremost in the trilby hat. *(Brian P. Jenkins)*

Policing the Cathedral City

Post-war, there was a preference for drafting disciplined men from the armed forces into Britain's constabularies, although some brought with them the terrible emotional and physical wounds suffered on the front. Although we know Cyril was wounded in 1918, he was fit enough to take the police oath and became the first post-war recruit for the Canterbury City Police in the early part of 1919. The Canterbury City Police was established on 7th March 1836 under the Municipal Corporations Act, although a system of paid night-watchmen had existed in the city from at least 1786. The municipal act created 178 democratic boroughs in England and Wales, each with a mandate for establishing a paid and regimented police force. Excluding Sir Robert Peel's Metropolitan Police of 1829, the municipal police are considered the beginning of conventional law enforcement in England and Wales.

When Cyril went for his interview with the chief constable, a chance encounter with PC Jim Butcher in Canterbury police station made him a friend for life. Seeing the elder constable walk by proudly wearing his Egyptian Campaign medals, Cyril was overcome with 'visions of majors and sergeant majors' and threw him a salute!

Canterbury East Station, 1919. PC Jenkins, left column, three back, found himself in the position of welcoming home the last of the Royal East and West Kent Regiment's troops. *(Brian P. Jenkins)*

The war had a profound effect on police forces. The sudden resignation of officers with patriotic inclinations left some of the small constabularies under strength, although they were soon able to boost their numbers by enlisting special constables and dividing them into first and second reserves. It was just so that one of those officers of the Canterbury force, a Police Sergeant Jack Ives, resigned and enlisted with the East Kent 'Buffs' as a Sergeant-Major Instructor. His police uniform and accoutrements were inherited by Cyril.

'Turning out' in Wincheap

Cyril's first shift – 'turning out' in the police vernacular – was on 16th February 1919, a night shift in the Wincheap area accompanied by PC Jesse Lockey. Policing in this era was a matter of covering almost every square-mile of the force's jurisdiction on foot. A 'conference point' system existed whereby constables stuck to predefined routes and met a sergeant or inspector at agreed points on the hour. Canterbury's method though was much stricter, taking in fifteen-minute points throughout the whole tour of duty. Missing a point, or abandoning a beat altogether, carried the threat of a dock in pay or even expulsion for frequent offenders.

Tail-end Charlie

The typical night turn comprised two sergeants and ten constables, who emerged from the police station and paraded in file down St. Peter's Road before each 'peeled off' to his respective beat. The last man in file, the 'tail-end Charlie,' carried a stout-stick indicating he was on boundary duty, taking in the winding back lanes and farms including Merton and Nackington Farms, the Gate Inn, Barton and Hoath Farms, the Polo Ground and Sanatorium. Being the only officer not required to meet a senior throughout the patrol it was prudent to prove he'd reached the boundary limit – noting how many patients were currently in the sanatorium was one method.

In the absence of any formal training, Cyril learned his craft from those around him. Young policemen often suffered jibes from local ne'er-do-wells eager to get a rise out of them and it was men like PC Harry Robinson, loose-limbed and powerful, who gave Cyril a practical demonstration while dealing with a couple of 'rowdies' at Nelson's Passage, Northgate. While we don't know precisely how the formidable PC Robinson impressed his experience upon PC Jenkins, it was a lesson that was passed on to successive recruits throughout Cyril's career.

It was important for a policeman to have a good knowledge of the borough's local miscreants and Cyril learned much from Detective Constable Alf Deal, an enthusiastic officer and born thief-catcher. He always stood up for the younger officers and encouraged them to 'have a go' when the situation dictated. Deal sadly died from tuberculosis shortly after his promotion to Detective Sergeant in late 1919.

30th September 1919. While still a probationer, Cyril wed Ethel Maud Jordan at St. Werburgh's Anglican Church in Hoo, Kent. Ethel was the daughter of a farm bailiff and was raised on a fruit farm on Church Lane, Molash, in Kent. *(Peter B. Jenkins)*

Constable number 9 Cyril Jenkins, 1919. The first post-war recruit of the Canterbury City Police. *(Brian P. Jenkins)*

Cyril's tutor in the early years was PC Bertie Inge. He lodged with his mentor at 8 New Street in St. Dunstan's while a probationer – a common practice for young unmarried constables. It was fortunate for Cyril that this arrangement was not a step into the unknown. PC Inge was married to Julia Jordan, one of his friend Bertie's sisters, and Cyril's association with the Jordan family was cemented when Cyril married Bertie and Julia's sister Ethel in Hoo on the Isle of Grain, Kent, on 30th September 1919. Ethel had been in Cyril's life for some years; sharing a trench with Bertie Jordan, Cyril helped him write home from the front and it was Ethel who received her brother's letters in Cyril's handwriting. In 1920, Bertie tragically died in a fall whilst working on Stone Pier, Stone, near Dartford.

Aspirations of leadership

As he settled into the police force, Cyril became ambitious for promotion – no easy feat in a small constabulary of only thirty-five men and it was a matter of waiting for other officers to retire in order to progress. Despite the challenges, Cyril was promoted to sergeant on 24th March 1924 and inspector on 18th July 1928 (the equivalent of Deputy Chief Constable.) Ever eager to expand his knowledge and influence, he was sent to London in 1927 and attached to the Metropolitan Police CID where he was tutored in criminal investigations. On return to Canterbury, he founded the force's first Criminal Investigations Department. It was during the latter years of the 1920s that Cyril was befriended by G.R. Hews, editor of the *Kentish Gazette* and city council alderman. It is to Mr Hews that Cyril owes his learning of shorthand, a skill Hews insisted would further his career.

His desire to advance through the ranks did not stop with the attainment of an inspectorship. In 1931, he applied for the chief constableship of Rochester City Police after the incumbent Mr Arnold retired through ill-health. The number of applicants was vast, and Cyril lost out to Herbert Allen, a chief inspector from Gravesend Borough Police. Allen remained in post for only two years, prompting Cyril to apply again. This time he lost out to Inspector H.P. Hind from the Nottingham Constabulary.

The proving grounds of Canterbury City moulded Cyril Jenkins into a fine police officer. It was where he learned his trade, came of age and became father to three children – Donald (1924) Marjorie (1926) and Roy (1928) – perhaps one of life's most challenging undertakings.

The chief constable, sergeants and inspectors, 1930. Photographed outside the entrance of Canterbury Cathedral. *(Brian P. Jenkins)*

1934. Inspector Jenkins escorting Mayor Frederick Lefevre and Town Clerk George Marks through the grounds of Canterbury Cathedral. *(Brian P. Jenkins)*

PC Bertie Henry Inge, c1930, at the St. Lawrence County Cricket Ground. The portly PC Inge was an early mentor to Cyril Jenkins. In 1921, Inge achieved some infamy in the Canterbury force for disarming 27-year-old William Richards on Broad Street. Richards, who Inge recognised as matching the description of a wanted thief, pulled a gun on him when challenged but soon found himself disarmed and under arrest. For his actions, Inge was awarded a pistol-shaped brandy bottle by his peers and spent his retirement years regaling the local bar flies with the story in exchange for a pint. Inge joined the Canterbury City Police on 20th July 1907 and retired on 31st August 1933. *(Robert D. Mott)*

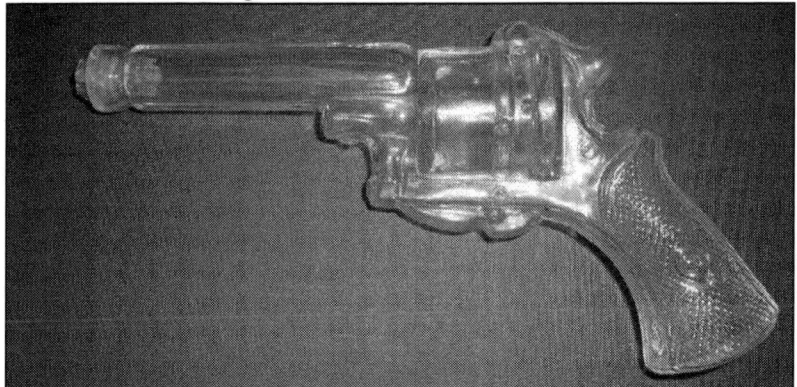

PC Inge and PC Port, c1930. Pictured here on New Street, St. Dunstan's in Canterbury. Port was another 11th Battalion veteran and lived next door but one to the Inge household. *(Robert D. Mott)*

The fruit of Inge's bravery was this pistol-shaped brandy bottle!

Canterbury City Police helmet plate. The coat of arms features a heraldic leopard and three choughs (birds of the crow family) taken from the arms of Thomas Becket. The Latin 'Ave Angliae Mater' translates 'Hail Mother of England.' *(PMCC)*

Inspector Jenkins in the 1930s. He was one of only two inspectors in the force, in the days when police inspectors were also deputy chief constables. *(Brian P. Jenkins)*

West to the Holy Headland

The Penzance Borough Police was formed on 1st January 1836. The head constable carried the archaic title of 'Le Yeoman,' borrowed from the borough's ancient charter bestowed in the year 1614. Harry Kenyon, only the fourth 'le yeoman' in 100 years, announced his decision to retire in November 1936 and worked his last day on New Year's Eve. Still eager to lead a force of his own, R.C.M. Jenkins applied for the chief constableship of Penzance and was successful, beating several local candidates to the post.

It was a small constabulary of twenty-four constables to a borough population of 19,827. Headquarters was located in the basement of the magnificent St. John's Hall municipal buildings on Alverton Street. Stepping into Kenyon's shoes however proved difficult in the early days. His predecessor was a well-established and influential socialite, known for throwing magnificent charity dances for the region's affluent in the ballroom at St. John's Hall every Christmas. When Jenkins took over, Kenyon insisted on remaining as inspector of weights and measures (normally an extraneous duty of the chief constable) and took immediate responsibility for raising Penzance's Auxiliary Fire Service (AFS,) another duty meant for the chief constable. Whether Kenyon's actions were done out of kindness to his successor during the settling-in period or were evidence of an unwillingness to let go of municipal affairs is unknown, and by 1939 Kenyon's influence had largely ebbed away leaving the latter responsibilities back in the control of Chief Constable Jenkins.

Chief Constable R.C.M. Jenkins, 1st January 1937. Jenkins was the first chief constable in the Penzance force to wear the new borough crest on the cap badge and lapels. *(Brian P. Jenkins)*

Old and new borough police crests. The old crest, worn since the force's inception in 1836, depicted the grim representation of St. John the Baptist's severed head on a charger. *(Simon Dell)*

Brass tunic button. Worn by Penzance officers 1836-1936.

"I'll take it from here." Jenkins takes over from Harry Kenyon, 1st January 1937. Photo taken on the steps of St. John's Hall. *(B.P. Jenkins)*

The sage experience impressed upon Cyril Jenkins as a young constable came in useful on the evening of 12th May 1937. The force on that night was concerned in keeping the peace during the celebration of King George VI's Coronation, and Penzance Town was alive with good cheer. Returning from a patrol of Wherrytown, Cyril saw two constables arguing with a drunk man outside the Winter Garden Hall. The man, George Thomas Bennetts, had been liberated from his employment as a waiter at the Winter Garden Hall only moments before having been caught drinking on the job. Refusing to accept his dismissal, the obstreperous Mr Bennetts took his anger out on the constables, who were struggling to make headway, forcing the chief constable to step in. Cyril first took Bennetts to one side, pleaded for calm, and asked him to go on his way. He ignored this advice and tried to barge past the chief constable, who stood firm in preventing him back into the hall. Bennetts then struck Cyril once in the chest, and was arrested for assault.

'I'll see you in court!'

Bennetts' arrest proved troublesome. He strongly resisted the application of handcuffs and was vocal all the way to the cells, where he was restless for much of the night. At sunrise, Bennetts continued his war of words with the Penzance force and demanded to see the chief constable in his office. Cyril agreed, and as he stormed into the room demanded the use of the chief constable's telephone so he could call his wife. Cyril calmly handed him the telephone handset, causing Bennetts to suddenly change his mind and loudly proclaim 'I'll see you in court!' He was later charged with assault and fined ten shillings.

Looe, Cornwall, 1941. The Wolseley motor car is Cyril's personal transport, bearing registration 'JG8403,' a Canterbury registry. *(BPJ)*

Penzance Borough Police. The entire regular force as it was in 1937. Taken on the steps of St. John's Hall. *(Simon Dell)*

A job well done. At the scene of a house fire in Newlyn, 1938. *(Brian P. Jenkins)*

A doting father. With son Roy on Penzance Promenade, 1938. The building on the right is now the Queen's Hotel. *(Brian P. Jenkins)*

Enjoying the sights. Mousehole Harbour, Cornwall, 1938. *(BPJ)*

The Policeman's Ball

The first charity ball under Cyril's leadership was held on 3rd December 1937, and was the first to take place in five years – Mr Kenyon had, for reasons unknown, declined to hold one since 1932. With Kenyon's encouragement, Cyril began preparing for the occasion in the latter half of November. Invitations went out to various high-ranking officials across the counties of Devon and Cornwall – mayors and mayoresses, chief constables of neighbouring police forces and their wives. Constables were permitted to sell tickets while on patrol, and in the days leading up to December 3rd the wives and children of Penzance's police force decorated St. John's Hall ballroom with Chinese lanterns, coloured lightbulbs and beautiful floral displays. Particular attention was paid to the ballroom stage; a linen backdrop depicting a country scene hung behind where Jerry Baker & His Orchestra would play, and a wooden trellis decorated with narcissus, chrysanthemums and coloured lightbulbs sat at the foot of the stage. The mirrored walls of St. John's Hall added infinite dimensions of opulence. Mr Kenyon naturally kept the festivities flowing from behind the scenes, and chaired a whist drive at the end of the evening with over 400 prizes awarded with the help of Mrs Jenkins. Cyril closed off the night with a rousing speech and a toast, promising a grander ball for 1938. That promise was kept and the following year over 500 were in attendance, the highlight of the night being the 'Lambeth Walk' dance with its signature 'Oi!' exclaimed at the appropriate juncture by hundreds of dancers. Cyril's closing speech promised an even grander ball for 1939, but that was a promise he could not keep. With the political situation in Europe untenable, the war clouds gathered once again and from 3rd September 1939, the force was set on a path from which it would never return.

Years of mandatory training left Cyril well-prepared for building Penzance's civil defence force, which was to consist of special constables, ARP wardens, the Auxiliary Fire Service, St. John's Ambulance Brigade and the unprecedented Home Guard. Any similarity to a certain British sitcom should have been coincidental, yet many years later he would tell his grandchildren that the exploits of Captain Mainwaring and his motley regiment were very true to real life!

The War Auxiliaries

On the day war was declared, Cyril put a call out for volunteers for the Penzance Special Constabulary. The response was overwhelming, with even the borough undertaker coming forward to form part of what became known as the Penzance Borough Police War Reserve. The building of the town's auxiliaries though was not without its troubles. Both the regular and auxiliary police forces of Penzance, and the Home Guard, received priority service for uniforms, leaving the ARP wardens disgruntled and unmotivated. In his capacity as ARP Sub-Controller, Jenkins reasoned that the Home Guard was more appealing to citizens of the borough, and in maintaining the interest of the wardens, 'the rattle in this instance is more important than the rifle.'

'There is a tremendous battle coming'

"We are in the war up to the hilt. We have to win this war and beat the Nazis, or they are going to beat us. We have to understand that. It is for the three fighting services to attack, and the best form of defence is attack. It is for them to punch as hard as they can. It remains for the civil defence workers to take the punches that are returned. These punches will be hard ones. Some of these will undoubtedly be below the belt. It is our task to stand up to that kind of attack. Twenty-odd years ago, we were doing our jobs. Today we are standing by to do our job again, supporting the younger fellows who are doing theirs. They are going to have a tough task. War brings out the weaknesses of the nation. Those who remembered the last war will have in mind the laxity of morals which occurred. This time we older ones can help to keeps things on an even keel.

THERE IS A TREMENDOUS BATTLE COMING; THERE IS NO DOUBT ABOUT IT. THE EVACUEES WILL BE COMING DOWN HERE AS SOON AS THE BOMBING STARTS. I BELIEVE THAT BOMBING WILL BE THE BEGINNING OF THE END. THE GERMANS WILL NOT STAND UP TO IT AS WE SHALL."[iii]

This speech, almost Churchillian in execution, was delivered by Chief Constable Jenkins to the Police Watch Committee in February 1940. Facing the second war in a lifetime was a troubling prospect. Cyril was still a child when he joined the colours in 1914, and now he had children of his own, and the responsibility of protecting Penzance weighed heavily on his shoulders. His eldest son Donald, too young to serve in the armed forces, volunteered for the Auxiliary Fire Service (which was now free from the influence of Harry Kenyon) with his father's blessing. The AFS's primary function was dealing with the aftermath of air raids, and Cyril dreaded sending Donald's unit out. Although his instinct was to protect, it was the chief constable's duty to send the unit to the worst raids.

On Sunday 17th March 1940, Cyril initiated a large-scale test run of Penzance's civil defence response. Numbering over 260 volunteers, the event was scrutinised by the County ARP Controller Major G.H. Johnstone, and Chief ARP Warden F.S. Shaw. Personnel included twenty umpires, twenty control room operators, one hundred AFS firefighters, ten decontaminators, ten medics, ten demolition workers, twenty messengers and the entire Penzance Borough Police force. Further participants included members of the local Boy Scout group, Air Cadets and seventy members of the community who acted as 'casualties.' Equipment included two fire engines, eight AFS pumps, four ambulances, five cars for treating casualties, a mobile first-aid post and three mobile water vans.

The Special Constabulary, 1940. An important war auxiliary, the officers wore the letters 'WR' on their tunics denoting they were part of the war reserve. *(Simon Dell)*

Inspection of the Penzance Borough Police War Reserves, 1940. The inspecting officer is Sir Charles Chitham, Acting Inspector of Constabulary. *(Brian P. Jenkins)*

Above & below. Parade and inspection of the AFS, 1940. *(B.P. Jenkins)*

The operation was a rousing success, drawing praise for the chief constable from all involved. Twenty 'incidents' were supervised, including a mock rescue operation at a derelict building on Coinagehall Street, an oil fire at Taylor's Garage and various demolition and decontamination exercises at sundry points. His ARP training had paid off. Nobody dreamed that the Luftwaffe would bother Penzance – commentators in the counties, principally local MPs unhappy at the amount of corporation money being spent on civil defence, thought that the Germans would never reach British airspace, because '…the RAF would intercept them!' The vocal minority would eventually have to eat their words, for in the summer of 1941 the peaceful skies over Penzance were broken by the rumble of enemy aircraft engines. On 2nd June 1941, bombs landed in the parishes of St. Clare and Gulval, with damaged caused to houses and electricity cables. The worst was to come however on 8th June, when ten high explosives and innumerable incendiary bombs rained on Penzance. Six houses on Alma Place were destroyed with a further thirty suffering serious damage. Another bomb landed in St. James Street, killing nine including a county police sergeant.

The war had come to Penzance

Donald Jenkins, centre-back row, West Cornwall Hospital, 1941. Wounded, but still smiling. His father's worries were confirmed when he was injured during the 1941 air raids on Penzance. *(Peter B. Jenkins)*

The war comes to Penzance. Ruined house with the spire of Lloyds Bank in the background, 1941. *(George Brown)*

The Blitz created a peculiar problem in Penzance – following the events of the 2nd and 8th June, residents from the borough began sleeping overnight in fields, barns and outbuildings where they believed it was safer. Although logical, complaints were made that public transport was not coping with the influx of residents returning en masse from the parishes after sunrise. Dealing with air raids was much more than a matter of coping with the aftermath. The adage 'prevention is better than cure' holds water, and why we find the police in wartime Penzance enforcing so-called 'Blackout Rules.' The rules, an absolute necessity in the eyes of the police and loathed by the public, were essential in minimising damage during night raids – simply, if the enemy couldn't see any light, then they could not accurately bomb their targets. The ARP were the primary enforcers of blackout rules, yet when it came to dealing with resistance to the regulations they had to call upon a constable, especially if it meant forcing entry to a house to extinguish an errant bulb or candle. Such matters were reported to the ARP Sub-Controller, normally a senior member of the corporation. In Penzance's case, it was the chief constable who carried out this role.

The seriousness of blackout offences can be evidenced from a session of the Penzance Police Court, held on 24th September 1940. Resident William Groves was hauled before magistrates for driving a motor vehicle with an improperly covered sidelamp, an indiscretion which cost him five shillings. Jenkins told Groves that he must immediately mend the lamp by 'covering with two sheets of newspaper or something of equal thickness to diffuse the light.' Fines went as high as £2 for rulebreakers and such was the problem in Penzance that, during the same court hearing, Alderman John Birch recommended an increase in the fine to £8 and even a custodial sentence for the most prolific offenders.

Bomb damage on Alverton Street, 1941. Further raids on 21st June and 18th and 23rd July provided similar ruin. The constable standing guard is one of the Cornwall Constabulary officers sent to assist the borough police. *(George Brown)*

As an old soldier, Cyril was acutely aware of the concept of the 'conscientious objector.' During the Second World War, many jobs in society were regarded 'reserved occupations' and men who were bakers, butchers or gas and electric workers were excluded from conscription. The office of police constable was also a reserved occupation, but for those with the First World War fresh in their minds, there were many misunderstandings. The sight of a police constable of conscription age on patrol often drew heckles and the 'white feather treatment.' Arrests were made more difficult by those wanting to have a pop at the younger men of the force, with many of them subject to extreme verbal abuse or assaults. It was a problem that infuriated Chief Constable Jenkins, and on 27th June 1940 he brought the matter before the Penzance Police Court:

"It has become increasingly prevalent by certain offenders when spoken to by the police to become abusive to the policeman, and young policemen are being asked 'why aren't you in the Army?' Young policemen are not in the Army because they are not allowed to join. It is the policy of the Government to retain trained men in their particular jobs, and no policeman can go into the Army no matter how much he wishes. It is not fair to these young men to have this thrown at them, and I would ask the persons making these remarks what they are doing."[iv]

The Forbes connection

A notable resident in this time was the artist Stanhope Alexander Forbes. Originally from Dublin, Forbes moved to the parish of Newlyn, near Penzance, in 1884 and became captivated by its charm and eclectic mix of residents. The region however was not completely alien to him – while honing his craft in Paris and Antwerp he saw many depictions of Newlyn on the canvasses of his fellow students.

By the time the Jenkins family arrived in Penzance, Forbes was a well-established pillar of the community. Having founded Newlyn Art School in 1899 with his wife Elizabeth, also an artist, he was the leading figure of a colony of artists to inhabit Newlyn and Penzance. While we don't know when Cyril and Stanhope first met, the bond was strong enough for the artist to become known as 'Daddy Forbes' among the Jenkins family, perhaps a contraction of Forbes' better known sobriquet 'The Father of the Newlyn School.'

Forbes inhabited a large house on high ground at Chywoone Hill which was supplied with electricity by a diesel generator in a wooden outbuilding. Some time before Christmas 1938, the building caught fire. Less than ten minutes after Forbes raised the alarm, Chief Constable

Jenkins had arrived with the entire Penzance Fire Brigade in tow. Known for its extensive thatched cottages, Newlyn was a hotspot for fires throughout the 1930s, with the last of its thatched roofs claimed by fire in 1938, making Forbes' paintings of the latter the few surviving depictions of Newlyn's quaint country cottages.

One year after the conflagration at the Forbes' estate, Forbes painted a stunning half-portrait of Cyril and showcased it at the Newlyn Society of Artist's Christmas Exhibition. A looser Forbes connection can be found in Effie James, a striking artist's model who was the subject of Frank Bramley's 1888 work 'A Hopeless Dawn' where she is seen as the woman kneeling in grief at her grandmother's lap. Effie modelled for others at the Newlyn School including Forbes. In 1944, Cyril's eldest son Donald married Effie's granddaughter, Effie Reynolds James, in the Parish of Gulval.

Immortalised on canvas. Painted by the Irish artist Stanhope A. Forbes in 1939, it was the centrepiece of the 1939 Newlyn Society of Artists' Christmas art exhibition. The piece remained in the care of the Jenkins family until Ethel's passing in 1987. *(Brian P. Jenkins)*

Stanhope A. Forbes RA. A resident of Newlyn when Cyril Jenkins was chief constable. *(Brian P. Jenkins)*

A cold reception on the Scillies

In 1941, the Government became interested in the policing arrangements on the Isles of Scilly, a rocky archipelago located 28 miles south-west of Land's End. Policing of the five inhabited isles had been conducted by parish constables throughout the ages, and invariably by its part-time policemen since at least 1861. The Second World War though brought big changes for policing, and the Home Office decided it could no longer leave the Scillies to its own devices.

At some point in 1941, the only full-time officer, Sergeant Eric Guy, resigned and joined the Navy, leaving the running of the police on Scilly to his subordinate, Constable Hurrell. The Home Office subsequently asked Jenkins to charter a vessel to the Scilly Isles to inspect the force in its current state and report his findings. Jenkins arrived at the island of St. Mary's in illustrious fashion, having obtained the services of a Royal Navy motor torpedo boat to make the journey! With the islanders accustomed to being free from the interference of the mainland, the sight of the Chief Constable of Penzance arriving like an invasion force was met with a cool reception. His remarks on the state of the force were damning:

"This service is one of the worst on the islands. The Sergeant has resigned and has not been replaced. The constable, an untrained man of nearly sixty years of age and with short police experience, now deals with policing matters. His position is exceedingly difficult unless he takes the line of least resistance."[v]

The situation was remedied by the temporary dispatch of a police sergeant from the Penzance Borough Police to the isles and in 1942, following scrutiny of Cyril's findings, the Cornwall Constabulary sent two officers to take over the running of the force, an arrangement made permanent by statute on 1st April 1947.

On 10th November 1941, the Chairman of the Police Watch Committee F.S. Shaw addressed the Corporation of Penzance and announced that Jenkins would be stepping down as chief constable to be appointed Chief Constable of the Folkestone Borough Police, in Kent. Jenkins made a lasting impression on the Penzance force. Paying tribute, Mr Shaw said:

"Soon after his appointment Mr Jenkins had reorganised the force and raised it to a high degree of efficiency. There was no force in the country working with greater efficiency than (the) Penzance Borough Force..."

Cyril modestly replied:

"*If I have achieved any measure of success, it is due to the willing co-operation I have received.*"[vi]

At the time this book went to print, nonagenarian Gerald Nicholls, a resident of Penzance, was able to offer a small recollection of an encounter with Cyril while he was chief constable. Gerald even his nineties is flamboyant and impulsive and he tells the story of applying in his youth at Penzance for his blasting licence and being ushered into the office of the chief constable, a position that wouldn't normally deal with this kind of paperwork. Gerald's character had obviously made enough of an impression on the constables for him to be 'wheeled in.' Gerald recalls quite clearly after pleasantries Cyril saying, 'you can have your blasting licence but don't blow your blooming legs off boy!'

Scandal in Hellfire Corner

In 1922, Chief Constable Harry Reeve stepped down from the Folkestone Borough Police and the Watch Committee appointed Alfred Beesley as his successor. This proved to be a disastrous move, for Mr Beesley soon revealed his true colours. Frequently rude towards the corporation and his subordinates, Beesley was incredibly stubborn and refused to wear uniform except for official functions. It is not known for how long Beesley was 'on the take,' but by 1941 an official complaint to the Watch Committee from a Police Sergeant Floydd shone a troubling spotlight on the chief constable.

The allegations were very damaging. Petrol coupons, a precious currency in ration era Britain, were being issued to unauthorised persons by the chief constable, including his own family members. Floydd further accused Beesley of using a police patrol car for his own personal use, and for allowing a police inspector to take a patrol car out of the county without good reason. Unfortunately for his accuser, the Watch Committee found no evidence against Beesley, and they were unable to issue any reprimand. Furthermore, when Beesley discovered whom his accuser was, he worked hard to make his life a living hell. Counter-allegations against the sergeant included taking a patrol car without permission and making false entries in a police log book. The Watch Committee found no evidence against the him, and a short time later Floydd made yet another complaint that Beesley was showing up for work drunk. Infuriated by the complaint, Beesley dismissed Floydd, an act that the Watch Committee refused to ratify. Floydd was reinstated immediately.

It came as an ironically welcome reprieve for the Folkestone Watch Committee when, in 1941, ex-constable Eric Morgan was arrested for committing a series of burglaries to dwellings and business premises. One of the force's own detectives, a Detective Constable Welch, had visited Morgan's home and looked through the window to see various items of property belonging to a Captain E.C. Shankland, reported stolen some time previous. The detective obtained a warrant and found further stolen property inside. Following his arrest, Morgan was amenable and wilfully acknowledged his crimes.

'What about the others?'

As Morgan was led away from court to a nine-month prison sentence, his wife cried from the gallery 'what about the others?' and accused a further thirteen officers of colluding with Morgan to commit large scale burglary since at least 1935. This gave the Watch Committee solid grounds to consider the chief constable's position untenable, and Beesley was asked to resign. The revelation that a small cabal of the Folkestone force were criminals forced the Watch Committee to call for help from the outside, and on 8th December 1941 Robert Cyril Morton Jenkins stepped in to sort out the mess.

Folkestone's geography meant it was well in range of Hitler's artillery guns and the dreaded 'Doodle-Bugs' – new and terrifying long-range rockets launched from the French and Dutch coasts. It is unsurprising that the boroughs of Folkestone, Dover and others became collectively known as 'Hellfire Corner,' requiring the full attention of the police and defence auxiliaries in protecting life and limb.

A force in total disarray could not possibly meet the demands of civil defence, and Jenkins needed help to chair an inquiry quickly and efficiently. That help was provided by the London Metropolitan Police, which sent two detectives from Scotland Yard to investigate the allegations. One of the officers, a Detective Inspector Hawkyard, interviewed Morgan in jail, and was passed the names of the alleged guilty. Writing in the *Police Review* in 1943, Chief Constable Jenkins discussed the outcome of the inquiry:

"I was able to secure the assistance of Det. Insp. Hawkyard and a sergeant... The Scotland Yard attitude was that after so much delay (the first of these offences is alleged to have occurred on July 31st 1935) it was most unlikely that sufficient evidence to justify criminal proceedings would be forthcoming, and that the efforts should be towards clearing the Force of the persons concerned. If criminal proceedings were instituted and they failed... it might then be difficult to deal with the person in a disciplinary manner. ...It was only after close and continued questioning that any admissions were obtained.

Ultimately the five constables... made statements in which they admitted committing felonious acts while on night duty... Sergeant Griffiths was alleged to have been concerned in certain cases... but... he strenuously denied the allegations. ...however I found... that he was unfit to remain in the force and I called for his resignation.... He resigned forthwith... Morgan had made certain allegations concerning five other men who are still serving in this force and after four days of exhaustive enquiry I was satisfied that there was no evidence whatever against any of these officers."[vii]

6 POLICEMEN SACKED AFTER INQUIRY

The exoneration of the Folkestone Borough Police was the unfortunate final chapter for the force, which was one of the municipal constabularies founded in 1836, and, save for the indiscretions of Beesley, Morgan and others it had a largely proud history. Following the scandal, Cyril refocused his efforts on civil defence and oversaw operations from the 'Report & Control Centre' located at the Town Hall on Rendezvous Street. In November 1942, he was injured in an air raid. News of his injury reached his old force in Penzance, and the officers and alderman of the corporation sent their well wishes.

Amalgamation

On 31st March 1943, Folkestone Borough Police was forcibly amalgamated with the Kent County Constabulary under directive from the Home Office. It was not a move unique to Folkestone – many city and borough police forces in England and Wales were required to temporarily amalgamate with the county forces to reduce the number of chief constables the military had to liaise with for civil defence. Under the *Defence (Amalgamation of Police) Act 1942*, the city forces of Canterbury and Rochester, and the borough forces of Dover, Gravesend, Margate, Ramsgate, and the Royal Borough of Tunbridge Wells merged, along with Folkestone, with the Kent County Constabulary creating a superpower in the south-east of England.

A Force for the County

At around noon on 10th October 1942, Chief Constable Captain J.A. Davison left Kent County Constabulary headquarters and headed into a wooded area near Maidstone. Shortly after, his body was discovered by a Police Inspector Wood with a gunshot wound to the head. There was much speculation as to the reasons behind Davison's suicide, including certain 'monetary' and 'disciplinary' matters, and an inquest chaired by Coroner W.H. Whitehead provided unsympathetically that the chief constable had taken his own life because his mind was 'deranged.' It was a shocking and inconvenient moment for the county police which was severely fatigued by war work.

On 1st March 1943, Percy Sillitoe of the Glasgow City Police was installed as chief constable. The indomitable Sillitoe was already well-known among police circles for introducing police radios in patrol cars, civilian staff and the mandatory retirement of a police constable after 30 years' service. To a lesser extent he is known for the introduction of the black and white chequered band seen on the modern police constable's flat cap. Based on the design seen on the Glengarry bonnets of the Scottish Army regiments, it became known as the 'Sillitoe Tartan' and was said to help the public distinguish the police officer from the postman or bus conductor. The amalgamation of Kent's police forces was a popular concept for Sillitoe and it was he who ensured its permanence in the region under the terms of the *Police Act 1946*. The chief constables of the defunct city and borough forces were invited to take subordinated ranks in the county force as an alternative to retirement with an increased pension. Cyril Jenkins was one of the five chief constables to accept and was appointed Assistant Chief Constable in charge of Number Three District comprising the Folkestone, Canterbury, Ashford and Margate Divisions. In 1944, Cyril was transferred to police headquarters in Maidstone.

The County Police at War

Kent County Constabulary was formed on 14th January 1857 by virtue of the *1856 County & Borough Police Act*. Comprising 222 constables for a population of 313,138, the strength of the force immediately after the Second World War amalgamation had almost quadrupled to 805 for a population of 628,236. Nobody anticipated the scale of devastation rained upon Kent from 1939-1945 but it cannot be said its police force was unprepared. Civil Defence training had formed part of standard police instruction in Kent since 1936 and a year prior the best was made of a 'passive defence air exercise' held in the South-East of England; a collusion between the force and other civic authorities achieved a near complete blackout across the county during what was perceived as a routine Royal Air Force exercise.

Timber and sandbags

As the war clouds gathered, a concerted effort to protect the police estate was enacted by the strengthening of stations and call boxes with timber and layers and layers of sandbags. Constables took instruction in combating gas warfare and impressed this experience on civilian instructors for the various local authorities. In April 1939, an emergency room was set up at headquarters to co-ordinate the ARP and other auxiliaries including the Police War Reserve and Special Constabulary.

The sounding of an air raid siren over Kent signalled the declaration of war on 3rd September 1939 and despite utterances of 'phoney war' abound, the police were busier than ever. It was said that during one of the first air raids on the county, a young constable took to using his police whistle to usher folk into shelter. Having never used the contraption before, he was surprised to find that when he brought it to his lips and blew hard, it didn't make a sound, for the whole thing was blocked with fluff!

Kent senior officers, 1946. L-R: ACC Fowler, DCC Palmer, CC Sillitoe and ACC Jenkins. *(Brian P. Jenkins)*

Kent's geographic location brought it well within range of German artillery fire from the French and Belgian coasts and, thanks to the meticulous record-keeping of Assistant Chief Constable R.C.M. Jenkins, the scale of devastation can be provided with mathematical precision. 10,880 civilians were injured during air raids, cross-channel shelling or as a result of the dreaded V-1 'Doodlebug' Flying Bomb – 1,924 of those casualties died from their injuries. 93 police officers were injured, of which 26 were killed. 500,000 incendiary bombs, 30,116 high-explosive bombs and 3,636 shells fell on the county during 10,140 instances of enemy action. 387 enemy aircraft and 1,203 allied aircraft crashed killing 297 and 595 allied airmen respectively.

Sir Percy Sillitoe, 1945. One of great reformers of British policing, Cyril served under Sillitoe for the remainder of the war. *(Brian P. Jenkins)*

Although enemy invasion was not at the forefront of many minds in 1939, by 1940 the realisation that Hitler meant business led to the establishment of a special branch at headquarters to counter espionage and tackle subversive activities. The control and monitoring of aliens became a tiresome task for the police and no foreigner was permitted to enter or leave Kent without a police permit. The problem was compounded by the sudden influx of Irish workers into Kent seeking work in the war industries. Add the swarm of military activity, training the Home Guard, erecting road blocks, ensuring the smooth movement of troops and equipment and taking thousands of enquiries from worried members of the public every day, the force had never been tested in such a way before nor since. The sudden arrival of over 250,000 people from Dunkirk at Kent's ports was unprecedented and the force was at the forefront of one of the most significant humanitarian crises of the war at that point.

Dambusters

Perhaps one of the most remarkable secrets kept by the British authorities was the proving grounds of the infamous 'bouncing bomb.' Inspector Charles Setterfield, a friend and colleague of Cyril's, co-ordinated with the military to make approximately one square mile of Herne Bay a top-secret test site for Operation Chastise. So successful was the police operation that the trials went undetected and the subsequent bombing of Germany's Moehne Dam on 16th May 1943 is regarded as one of the defining moments of World War Two.

With Chief Constable Sillitoe heavily committed with many aspects of war work, it was left to ACC Jenkins to handle security matters in Kent and he met regularly with Prime Minister Winston Churchill at Chartwell. Cyril became well-acquainted with Churchill and on one occasion passed his wife Ethel's well wishes to the Prime Minister when they greeted. After the meeting, Churchill gave him a signed copy of his latest book to which Cyril said, 'thanks very much.' Churchill replied, 'It's not for you – it's for your wife!'

Stand down and thanksgiving

On 16th September 1945, Cyril joined the combined regular and auxiliary Kent County Constabulary at All Saints Church in Maidstone for an official 'stand down' parade and thanksgiving service. During the service, Cyril overheard a reserve policeman tell Chief Constable Sillitoe that he'd 'been in (the special constabulary) since the start.' Cyril quipped, 'then you must be very old!'[viii] referring to the ancient existence of the auxiliary force, raised during the reign of King Charles II of England.

Six long years of war had exhausted the combined Kent force which had come together for the common good and defended the county with valour. The force however was undeterred in its mission, and marched forward from the ashes of ruin invigorated by the leadership of its new chief constable Major John Ferguson after Percy Sillitoe departed in 1946 to become keeper of the nation's secrets at MI5.

On 1st January 1946, Cyril was awarded the King's Police & Fire Services Medal for Distinguished Service and in 1949, the King's Police Medal for Conspicuous Dedication to Duty. Further decorations included becoming a Serving Brother of the Venerable Order of Saint John on 1st January 1950 and, in the 1953 New Year Honours, R.C.M. Jenkins was made an Officer of the British Empire (O.B.E.)

Following the sudden death of Deputy Chief Constable William C. Palmer in 1947, Cyril was appointed Deputy Chief Constable on 22nd April of that year.

Despite the certainty of Hitler's defeat, the desire to maintain a strong civil defence force in Kent and indeed other police forces meant for many years the reserve and special constabularies were kept at substantial strength. On 1st April 1950, Cyril was the honoured guest at a dinner for the Special Constabulary 'L' Division at the San Clu Hotel in Ramsgate. Flanked by Assistant Chief Constable Fowler, Special Constabulary Commandant Major J. Robinson and Alderman Owen Hughes, the Mayor of Ramsgate, Cyril praised the hundreds of specials in attendance but spoke of the 'tragedy' that forces were still training in civil defence, even after two world wars. After joking that he always thought the borough officers were 'better' than the county police, and was sure the feeling was mutual, Cyril passed to Special Constabulary Divisional Commander Mr W.W. Lance Almond who thanked the volunteer force for committing over 30,000 hours of work over the preceding twelve months.

As Deputy Chief Constable, Cyril was senior co-ordinator for all major incidents in the county including the police response to the sinking of the T-Class submarine HMS Truculent in the Thames Estuary after leaving Chatham on 12th January 1950, the 'Siege of Symons Avenue' which saw the killing of PC Alan Baxter by gunman Derek Pooley, and the Gillingham bus crash of 4th December 1951, which killed twenty-four members of the Royal Marines Volunteer Cadet Corps as they marched in thick fog near Chatham Dockyard. Known as a strict disciplinarian, he was also in charge of force discipline.

The devastating floods on the Isle of Sheppey in February 1953 was another major operation for Cyril as DCC and earned the aforementioned Inspector Setterfield a B.E.M. for his quick thinking in the face of an unprecedented tidal surge that brought misery and ruin to thousands on the north-east coast of the county.

On 12th March 1952, Cyril was appointed Acting Chief Constable of the Newport Borough Police in South Wales. He arrived in Newport in the aftermath of a scandal (not a new experience!) The previous chief constable, Clifford Montague-Harris, was asked to resign following several instances of misconduct. Cyril though did not chair any inquiry as he did in Folkestone. Rather, his presence appears to have been as overseer until Chief Superintendent Smeed, also from Kent County Constabulary, was appointed permanent chief constable of Newport on 27th April 1952.

Police HQ, 1950. R.C.M. Jenkins, Major Ferguson C.B.E. (chief constable) and Inspector Keech. *(Brian P. Jenkins)*

Memorial unveiling, 1949. Major John Ferguson unveils the Kent County Constabulary war memorial at Maidstone HQ. *(BPJ)*

Foreign friends, 21st July 1951. Officers from Brussels City Police pay their respects at the HQ war memorial. *(Brian P. Jenkins)*

Memorial service, 21st July 1951. *(Brian P. Jenkins)*

Inspection of the Newport Borough Police, 1952. Jenkins, pictured here with HMI Tarry and Chief Superintendent Smeed (far left,) was appointed T/CC of Newport on 12th March 1952. *(Brian P. Jenkins)*

New Year Honours, 1953. Ethel, Cyril and their daughter Marjorie at Buckingham Palace when Cyril was awarded his O.B.E. *(Peter Jenkins)*

Award ceremony, 1953. Cyril presents the Campbell Cup to Miss M. Pay of the St. Paul's Young People's Fellowship. *(Brian P. Jenkins)*

1954. During a visit of the Inspector General of the Nigeria Police to Police Headquarters, Sutton Road, Maidstone. *(Brian P. Jenkins)*

1953. Jenkins, right, with Captain Griffiths, the ACC of the City of London Police. As well as being a crack-shot at the Canterbury City Rifle Club, Cyril was a keen golfer, bowler and cricketer. *(B.P. Jenkins)*

Police HQ Sports Day, 1955. Cyril and Ethel Jenkins greeting HRH Princess Alexandria. *(Brian P. Jenkins)*

Force inspection, 1961. Jenkins and Lord Cornwallis at HQ. *(BPJ)*

The Growing of the Apple

1957 saw developments that would shape the future of Cyril's family; a new house, an investment in a fruit farm, and the death of a son-in-law. In 1948, the family had moved from the Red House in Turketel Road, Folkestone, to live at Branksome, 40 Buckland Hill, in Maidstone. Cyril and Ethel desired to settle for future retirement having lived in many police houses over the years and thus, a plot was purchased at Bearsted on the corner of Ashford Road and Roseacre Lane. The new detached house, built to Cyril's specification, was designed by his eldest son Donald. Although it was always thought his sons Donald and Roy would make excellent policemen, they chose much different career paths. Donald became a Chartered Engineer and Roy became a fruit grower. The house featured an English Oak staircase and much hand-carved furniture made by W.C. Beaney, a local master craftsman.

Marjorie Jenkins had married and settled at Tonbridge with two young children. Her husband Roy Taylor was from a Folkestone family and was the son of H.C. Taylor, a stockbroker in the City of London. He followed his father in business and was made a partner in the firm of Simon and Coates Stockbrokers. On 4th December 1957, both the elder and younger Taylor caught the Ramsgate train from Cannon Street Station to

Tonbridge and Folkestone but were seated in different carriages. At 1820 in thick fog, disaster struck when the British Rail train struck another train at St. John's in Lewisham. Roy was killed, and thereafter with Marjorie widowed Cyril and Ethel would do what they could to help the family. Marjorie later joined Kent County Constabulary as a control room operator.

Roy Jenkins had studied fruit growing at the Kent Farm Institute and was employed in the industry as a pack house manager at Paddock Wood. He was ambitious to further his involvement in the industry and with the backing of his parents purchased the Castle Farm Estate, formerly owned by Hernden Farms Ltd, at Hadlow by auction. The much-told story is that as the bidding reached its climax, Ethel gave Cyril a nudge to encourage one more bid. At the fall of the gavel it was Cyril who bought the orchards at Court Lane for £7,500.

The sixty-three acres of orchards at Court Lane Farm, part of the Castle Farm Estate, was planted with apples and came with a pair of Victorian cottages. A trading company was formed, R.C. Jenkins Ltd, with Cyril, Ethel and Roy as founders and an agricultural mortgage put in place to finance the venture. The established orchards were planted with traditional standard, half-standard and bush trees on vigorous root stocks. Culinary varieties included Early Victoria, Grenadier and Bramley Seedling. Desert varieties included Beauty of Bath, Millers Seedling, Worcester Pearmain and Cox's Orange Pippin.

Cyril helped to oversee the development of the farm with the building of a road, farm buildings, cold storage facilities and a farmhouse. The farmhouse was designed by Donald Jenkins and completed in 1960. The family business made good progress with Cyril as a director who looked after the banking, book-keeping, insurance and strategy. Over the years the farm buildings and cold storage facilities were extended and the orchards improved with inter-planting of more commercial fruit varieties.

Roy Jenkins, c1950. Pictured here with his wife Kathleen Ann 'Kitty' (left) and his mother Ethel. *(Brian P. Jenkins)*

Donald Bertie Jenkins, 1944. Donald returned to Cornwall in 1944 to marry Effie Reynolds James in the Parish of Gulval, near Penzance. He followed in his father's footsteps and joined the Army, serving in Burma, and is seen here carrying the rank of captain with the Royal Engineers. *(Peter B. Jenkins)*

Marjorie Jenkins. Photograph taken at the gate of 'The Red House' at Turketel Road in Folkestone in the 1940s. *(Peter B. Jenkins)*

R.C.M. Jenkins retired from the Kent County Constabulary on 16th May 1963 after 44 years' service, with an exemplary record. He served 16 years as DCC of Kent, a feat unlikely to be repeated. In retirement, he wrote articles for the *Kentish Gazette* reflecting on his career in the Royal West Kent Regiment and Canterbury City Police. He was a keen sportsman, and spent much of his time away from home enjoying bowls, golf and cricket, often competing against or spectating with his surviving war comrades.

'Sandgate Passout' 1962. An inspection of new constables at the number 6 District Training Centre in Sandgate. Cyril was Acting Chief Constable in this time following the sudden death of the incumbent Geoffrey White. The police constable he is talking to is Robert D. Mott, his own great-nephew. The story goes that Cyril stopped and spoke to Mott about his service medals, not realising until later he was speaking to his relative. *(Robert D. Mott)*

Jim Jenner, Detective Chief Superintendent and a long-time friend and colleague, wrote an ode to Jenkins and read it aloud at his retirement party. The poem, titled 'Full Circle,' comprises eleven verses and has been reproduced in the following pages.

Full Circle

He started as a farmer, this stalwart son of Kent and then became a soldier though that was not his bent, for he joined as a trooper and ended up unhorsed, but still the love of uniform, through his veins it coursed.

So in Chaucer's pilgrim city, he donned his blue and argent, and as he wrote in shorthand, they stepped him up to sergeant, his prospects then were meagre – so with this he came to grips, by shooting his inspector, and picking up his 'pips.'

And then he travelled westwards, his prospects to enhance, and got himself appointed the 'cc' of Penzance, crossed batons on his shoulder, in Gilbert's pirate place, did not appease ambition, and so he set his face.

Back towards his homeland, and went to Folkestone boro where he dealt with poaching gamekeepers in manner prompt and thorough, now about this time in Whitehall in

Glasgow and Berlin certain things were stirring – to some 'cc's' chagrin.

The autonomy of small towns – was in the melting pot, and all the policemen in our county became one single lot. 'Amalgamate' t'was what they said and sent Sir Percy here, to mix us up, to integrate and mingle far and near.

So now our worthy Folkestone Chief, controlled a bigger zone. And soon came to the Kremlin[6] to sit next to the throne, a 'DCC' at 'HQ' he reigned for many a year. And every weekly order – brought forth its cheer or tear.

Promotions and removals were published by the score, the former caused the cheering – and the latter victims swore. He saw them come – he saw them go 'cc's – one, two and three. 'PJ', Sir John, and Geoffrey White and still he stayed to see.

Himself, made up, appointed, to be our acting chief, at a time when help was needed to tide us o'er our grief. Then came the next 'cc' from Hants[7] – yes he served yet one more boss, but now his time has come to go and sad will be our loss.

---

[6] The Soviet-style architecture of Maidstone HQ earned it the nickname 'Kremlin' and its occupants the 'polit bureau.'
[7] Following the sudden death of Geoffrey White, Cyril was A/CC until the appointment of Sir Richard Dawnay Lemon as CC in 1962.

For he was a policeman extraordinary – Kent's longest serving cop, he started at the bottom – he ended at the top. One job for him is over and to pension now he'll stop, our worthy friend and counsellor – 'Old Jenks' the County 'Dep.'

He's earned a rest from labour – but now will strive and grapple with the mysteries of finance and the growing of the apple.

Plums and pears and stocks and shares – replace crooks and crimes. The Discipline Regs are set aside and he reads the *Financial Times*. And so the wheel turns over for one unusual man, he started as a 'son of soil' and ends as he began.

Jim Jenner, 1963.

Deputy Chief Constable Jenkins, 1960. Note the absence of the bath star on the epaulettes which was not ascribed to the DCC until many years later. *(Kent Police Museum)*

R.C.M. Jenkins

O.B.E., K.P.M, S.B, O St. J

16th February 1919 – Joined Canterbury City Police as a constable.

1st January 1937 – Chief Constable of Penzance.

8th December 1941 – Chief Constable of Folkestone.

1st April 1943 – Assistant Chief Constable of Kent.

22nd April 1947 – Deputy Chief Constable of Kent.

12th March 1952 to 27th April 1952 – Acting Chief Constable of Newport.

17th October 1961 – Acting Chief Constable of Kent.

16th May 1963 – Retired from the police after 44 years' 89 days' service.

In 1969, the farm mortgage was paid off and progress on the farming business was good, however by the end of that year, Roy Jenkins' health failed and he passed away in December. The funeral that Christmas Eve saw Cyril stand and undertake the reading of Roy's Last Will and Testament. Now in his early seventies, Cyril took on the role of chairman of the business until the next generation were old enough, since Roy's children were all of school age.

He engaged capable staff to undertake the work including Hadlow Agricultural College-trained David Smith as manager and Jack Elphick, an experienced fruit man. Smith had been tutored by Charles 'Charlie' Brown, the farm manager at Boormans Farm, who had years prior also tutored Roy Jenkins at Borden, near Sittingbourne, when Hadlow (instituted in 1967) was known as the Kent Farm Institute. Cyril took advice from Charlie Brown over the years and realised that modernisation of the orchards and systems was required to ensure the farm's future commercial viability. Old orchards were grubbed and new planted with intensive tree systems on modern dwarfing root stocks including MM106, M26 and M1X types. Old varieties were replaced with more up to date types including Discovery, Spartan and more Cox's Orange Pippin. Handling systems were improved with the purchase of a tractor mounted forklift and pallets to reduce the hard labour.

R.C.M. Jenkins died on 18th March 1973, aged 74, from a heart condition, at 109 Ashford Road in Bearsted, Kent. The funeral took place at Bearsted Church near Maidstone, arranged and funded by Kent County Constabulary. One of the uniformed pallbearers was Police Sergeant Robert D. Mott, his great-nephew. Said to have been a man of high dedication, good moral fibre and virtuous humour, he was affectionately known by those close to him as 'Jenks' and 'Gramps' to his grandchildren, Ethel Jenkins survived her husband and all her children. She passed away in Tunbridge Wells in 1987.

A fateful gesture

Although Cyril was said to have been unconcerned about his own legacy, the donation of an oil painting to the chief constable of Devon and Cornwall Police, as per the terms of his Last Will and Testament, was a fateful gesture forty years in the making. It was this painting that started this author's fascination with Robert Cyril Morton Jenkins, and with the help of those who knew him it has been possible to tell his story.

Chief constables past and present. Devon & Cornwall Police Chief Constable Shaun Sawyer with the restored Forbes painting, Police HQ, Exeter. *(Mark Rothwell)*

Remembering Uncle Cyril

By Robert D. Mott

R.C.M. Jenkins, or 'Uncle Cyril' as he was known in our family, married my grandmother's sister Ethel Jordan and lived with my grandparents in St. Dunstan's in Canterbury for a while after joining Canterbury City Police. He was tutored by my grandfather, PC Bertie Inge.

My parents moved from Canterbury in 1938 after they were married, my father having joined the Windsor Borough Police Force in 1936. So, Uncle Cyril and Aunt Ethel were visited in Kent infrequently by my parents. My own first recollection of him was in 1952 when he and Ethel were returning from a caravan holiday in Cornwall. They called in to see us when we were living at Berkshire police headquarters on high ground at Sulhamstead near Reading. Uncle Cyril was towing the caravan with his own car fitted with a Kent Police Radio. I was with my father at the front of Police headquarters in the car as Cyril called up Kent Police Headquarters, hoping that the high ground would enable him to radio to Kent HQ. I recall that although we could hear the Kent transmissions, they could not hear his, so after a while he gave up.

When I applied to join Kent County Constabulary at the end of my R.A.F. service in 1962, my father, unknown to me, wrote to Uncle Cyril a personal letter to say that I had applied to join the force after 5 years in the RAF. It never reached him. It was intercepted and put in my file without him seeing it. He was Acting Chief Constable at the time and no doubt someone decided that he need not see it.

The next time I saw Uncle Cyril was at my passing out parade from the 6 District Training Centre at Sandgate near Folkestone in August 1962. These parades were reviewed by Chief Constables of the District on rotation. It happened to be Kent's turn and he was the Acting Chief Constable, so he it was who carried out the review. Before marching past the saluting base, the reviewing officer would walk down the ranks and speak to several of the officers that came to his attention. When he came to me he stopped, I do not think my name badge registered, but the fact that I was a Kent officer and that I was wearing a General Service Medal for service in Cyprus caught his attention and as you would expect, a brief formal question and answer session followed before he moved on.

My next, and final, meeting with him was in 1965 at the High Street junction with Guildhall Street in Canterbury. At that time, all the London to Dover traffic would travel through the heavily congested High Street.

The traffic lights at his junction were notorious for not operating properly; officers were issued with keys to operate the light manually. On just one such occasion I was getting the traffic moving again by manually operating the lights when Uncle Cyril saw me as he was walking from the Westgate Towers (and police station) direction towards St. Georges Street, and he made a point of standing next to me talking about the police, Canterbury City and my family whilst I was doing this. We talked for some time. As things improved I switched the traffic lights back on to automatic and he rightly said that I had better go to my next task! So, my last recollection of him is in a smart suit and brown trilby with a military bearing walking in the direction of St. Georges.

In 2013, I called in to the Kent Police Museum to say farewell to the curator, Anna Derham, on the museum's closure and leaving the post. I mentioned the photograph of R.C.M. Jenkins, and the photograph of the portrait of him by Stanhope Forbes. By coincidence, she had had a recent enquiry from someone in Devon & Cornwall Police, who turned out to be Mark Rothwell. Thus, it is thanks to Mark that the family and I now know so much more about R.C.M. Jenkins and his police career. It makes for compelling reading.

Some Reminiscences – Canterbury's Police Force of 50 Years Ago

By R.C.M. Jenkins

(The following is transcribed from the *Kentish Gazette*, as written by R.C.M. Jenkins for its 19th June 1964 issue.)

Recently 'Gazetteer' made the point in his columns that many present-day readers did not know that, until 1943, a Canterbury City Police Force existed. Although the following correspondence and comment showed that some of your older readers had neither forgotten that small force nor some of its members, the time is coming when that will no longer be the case.

During this year will fall the 50th anniversary of '1914 and all that,' and thus provide an outstanding opportunity of remembering those 'guardians of the peace' who patrolled the streets of the city before the outbreak of the 'Kaiser's War' and during those four years which followed – four years of constant fighting and tragic loss of life and limb, with their legacy of pain and suffering still being endured by some. The changes then brought about are now history, almost ancient history! It seems right, therefore, for 'Elder Citizens,' while there is yet time, to place on record aspects of city life of which they have particular knowledge.

It was my privilege, in early 1919, to be accepted as the first post-war recruit in the City Force, and therefore each and every one of my earliest police colleagues had been serving in the City Police by 1915-19, for recruiting had then ceased.

Who were these men? What did they do? How well were they known by the citizens? The strength of the City Police in 1914 was 35 all told – a Chief Constable, two Inspectors, five Sergeants and 27 Constables.

Who were they?

Chief Constable was Mr J.H. Dain, to whom reference has recently been made in these columns. Having served in several Forces, he came from Devonport to Canterbury where he quickly made his present felt. He was later appointed to Norwich, where he served for many years and became extremely well-known for his work and great interest in boys' clubs.

Inspectors Swain and Smith: 'Dick' Swain retired during the war and was later very well-known as an agent for the King's Proctor. An astute man, he was eminently suitable for confidential work of that nature.

'George' Smith served until 1928. For years he was the only Inspector in the Force. I can say from experience that he well knew how to keep the constables, especially the 'youngsters,' in order! At cricket matches and other outings he would readily join in the fun, but woe betide anyone who tried to take advantage on the following day.

Sergeants Ives, Jury, Ewell, Robinson and Parker: 'Jack' Ives retired shortly after the outbreak of war and returned to his old regiment, The Buffs, as a Sergeant-Major Instructor. No doubt his direct and forceful manner had a profound effect upon many of 'Kitchener's Mob,' as they were so pleased to call themselves. It so happens that my first police uniform was that handed in by Sergeant Ives.

'Charlie' Jury was for many years 'Plain Clothes' Sergeant – as he was then called. I remember him as a quiet resolute man, utterly trustworthy. The Magistrates, and in particular the Clerk (Mr T.A. Bowen) often made clear their reliance upon his testimony.

'Harry' Ewell was another man of high principles, who always strove to do his job fairly and to give encouragement to recruits. No matter how much we irritated him, we just could not drive him to any language stronger than 'messing about,' but the emphasis which he could put into those words was surprising!

'Harry' Robinson was a loose-limbed powerful man. Early in my service he gave me excellent advice upon handling some of our 'customers' who delighted in taking 'the rise' out of young policemen. On one particular occasion when we were dealing with a couple of rowdies in Nelson's Passage, Northgate, he gave me a practical demonstration which I never forgot – an in due time passed on to other young policemen.

'Alf' Parker became quite a crony of mine. He was a good practical policeman, but always a farmer at heart. His love for his home 'up on the Minnis' was obvious. Over a period of four years he was my sergeant. The next four years we shared a section as sergeants. Finally, I was his Inspector for four years – he could fairly claim, as he did when he retired, to know me from all angles!

Constables: I first refer to four, who, although constables in 1914, were promoted to sergeant's ranks either during or immediately after the war. They were PC's Richardson, Deal, Cole and Richards.

'Lew' Richardson was a man of equable temperament. He eventually became Detective Sergeant, and in that rank served until 1928. It was during his years that we really began to 'know' our County Police neighbours in Kirby Lane. Many people will recall him as County Court bailiff and an enthusiastic bowler.

'Alf' Deal was quite a character and a born thief-catcher. He had a tremendous knowledge of local 'ne'er-do-wells' and was always ready to instruct and advise young policemen who were energetic and ready to 'have a go.' Unfortunately, shortly after promotion to Detective Sergeant in 1919, he died of tuberculosis.

'Tom' Cole was quietly able – never one to hit the high spots but very dependable. I recall that he hailed from Faversham and had been a bricklayer.

'Bill' Richards is the only one of the foregoing who is still with us. A native of Sussex, he had served in 'The Heavies.' How many now know of the Blue Marines – the former Royal Marine Artillery? I once heard Bill Richards described (and I hope that this will not embarrass him) as 'one of God's Own.' I would neither quarrel with that description nor seek to add anything to it! I would merely thank him for his help and kindness over the years. Although now in his 80s, his carriage and deportment, whether walking or riding his cycle, would be a credit to many men of half his age.

The remainder of the constables of that era I would classify in three groups – The Old Group, The Middle Group and The Young Group. Little did they realise that the first would not be taking their pensions as they had thought; that a goodly proportion of the second group, and all of the third, would soon find themselves engaged in warfare while wearing uniform of a different colour!

The Old Group

'Bob' Stone, an old soldier, retired in 1914 and returned to the Royal Engineers where he became a 'pigeon man' and an expert of the then most important 'Pigeon Post.'

'Bill' Holness, who had earlier left the same village as myself (Stalisfield) to become a policeman, regularly worked the High Street point and there learned practically all that was going on in the city. There was time to stand and stare, also to talk, in those days!

'Jim' Butcher, another old soldier, who wore among his medals the Egyptian Star, was on duty at the police station when I called for interview. I was in khaki and, seeing that he wore a crown, I had visions of Majors and Sergeant Majors. Playing for safety, I threw him a smart salute and so made him a friend for life!

'Jim' and 'Ted' Goddard were brothers, good humoured to all and sundry except to each other, for, like so many brothers, they were every ready to argue with each other.

George, or 'Josh,' Reynolds was a quiet humourist who in later life ran his sweet shop at the corner of Station Road West.

'Bert' Orman, probably the biggest man in the Force, had served in the 1st King's Dragoon Guards. Like so many of his colleagues, he was a gardening enthusiast. He later worked in the beautiful gardens of Mr Richmond-Powell in Old Dover Road.

'Jesse' Lockey, ex-3rd Dragoon Guards, was, like myself, one of the smaller policemen. He was always precise and correct in speech and bearing. In later years, he was well-known as scorer for St. Lawrence and other cricket clubs. He initiated me to beat patrol on Wincheap beat on the night of Sunday, February 16, 1919, when I first 'turned out' without training of any kind.

The Middle Group

'Harry' Scoones used to supply the local Force with Metropolitan Police gossip, gleaned while on leave with his policeman brother.

'Walter' Maple, a member of the Harbledown family well-known for their cricketing prowess, was a tower of strength to the Police side. I often wonder how and why promotion passed him by, for he was a good copper!

'Bert' Inge, another stalwart, had served in the British South African Police, who, curiously enough, served in Rhodesia, not South Africa. It was he who 'showed me the ropes' more than any other person. It is a pleasure to me to see one of his grandsons[8] serving in the County Force at Canterbury.

'Ted' Lawrence and 'Jack' Ede were both former members of the 7th Dragoon Guards and their names were always coupled in Police circles. Both were soon to find themselves in France, in identical ranks – Sergeant Majors – of the Mounted Military Police. Both served with

---

[8] Robert D. Mott

distinction. Ted Lawrence, who is still with us and another G.O.M., was awarded both the D.C.M. and the M.M.; Jack Ede, a cool customer if there ever was one, was Mentioned in Despatches.

'Fred' Finn, who had been a 'looker' (shepherd) in the Romney Marsh area, was another who merited consideration for promotion. He was a most tenacious policeman and was, in consequence, a thorn in the side of habitual wrongdoers. He still enjoys his well-earned pension.

'George' Simpson was a quiet well-disposed man. He played better cricket in braces and other unorthodox 'rig' than many who were immaculately turned out. We often had cause to thank him for his high flighted 'lobs' of the Tich Freeman style.

'Charlie' Austin was another Buff. His energy in working his beat was as noteworthy as was his aversion from pen and ink. He often handed out summary justice rather than write a report.

'Gibe' Gibson parted company with the Force in the early 20s and, I believe, made far more money than had he stayed. I always felt that he was harshly dealt with for a trivial omission. However, there was no appeal against

Watch Committee decisions in those days – a most unsatisfactory state of affairs, now rectified.

'Harry' Culver, an amusing fellow, emigrated to Canada in the 20s. He could never get the hang of the *Daylight Saving Act*. One year he got into trouble for not altering his clock and in consequence parading an hour late. The next year he duly altered his clock and paraded two hours late! He had put it back instead of forward!

The Young Group

'Harry' Stapleton was 'Boss Man' of this section. During the war he was to serve in the R.A.M.C. and be taken prisoner. In later years, he became a sergeant in the Force. He and I always got on well – except at election times!

'Bert' Matson, a local man formerly with the S.E. and C.R.,[9] soon found himself in France with the Royal Field Artillery. He used to get intensely annoyed when we members of the P.B.I.[10] referred to his former unit as 'The 10-mile Snipers.' We were later to swap many a yarn in a sheltering doorway in the 'small hours.'

---

[9] South Eastern & Chatham Railway Company
[10] P.B.I. – 'Poor Bloody Infantry!'

'Reg' Goldfinch, who came from Deal, soon had a good look at the Eastern Mediterranean while serving with the R.A.M.C. He always maintained a quiet demeanour and was, I believe, at times shocked by his sometimes-hilarious comrades.

'Charlie' Ewell, younger brother of Sgt. H. Ewell, and 'Frank' Jordan soon joined that wealthy corps A.S.C (M.T.)[11] receiving 6/- per day for their services as drivers, whereas we 'footsloggers' got but 1/- per day! Our general moan was they got 6/- per day for bringing shells up the line, while we mugs in the line got 1/- for having them lobbed back at us! Both these fellows left the Force to set up in business in their own account. After a very sticky start they did well and the name of one is carried on by his family in a thriving city business today.

War Time Recruits

Before police recruiting ceased at the end of 1914 three other recruits came along, and after a few months found themselves in the Army.

'Oliver' Price, from Blean, went to Gallipoli with the R.E.K. Yeomanry and returned with a fund of stories about certain regimental characters well-known to both of us.

---

[11] Army Service Corps (Military Transport)

'Bert' Webb, from Merton Farm, and 'Bert' Kemp from a County Police family, soon departed to the Corps of Military Police and returned to police duty only after I had joined in 1919.

Bert Webb had an abrupt initiation to active service. Having been on traffic duty in Canterbury one weekend, he found himself the following weekend – having joined the Army on the Monday – sorting out Army convoys in Ypres Square, with plenty of heavy 'ironmongery' falling about to make the job interesting!

These then were the men who formed the City Police Force of 50 years ago. They had little or no training except that which they picked up in the hard school of experience. Their 'classrooms' were at such places as the Cattle Market on Saturday afternoons when the dealers and gypsies were showing off their horses; Northgate on Saturday nights; Military Road when units or drafts were due to go overseas on the morrow; or, of a different nature, on the following court day, undergoing cross-examination by such doughty advocates as the late Mr A.K. Mowll, Mr Walter Shea, or in the then infrequent motoring case, Mr Cuthbert Gardner.

Having joined the local Force, with but few exceptions, they patrolled the city on foot for 25 to 30 years and, in consequence, accumulated much detailed knowledge of businesses and families which extended over two or more generations. Those of us who followed in the early years after the war were fortunate in that we were able to shape and build our police careers upon the foundations laid by each and all of those to whom I have referred.

What Did They Do?

In 1914, apart from the plain clothes sergeant (as he was then termed) and an occasional constable in the station, engaged on cleaning or clerical work, there were no specialists. All ranks patrolled the streets on foot. The sergeants and constables were divided into two sections, day and night. The day section was again divided by two, early and late turn, i.e., early turn 6 a.m. to 10 a.m., 2 p.m. to 6 p.m.; late turn 10 a.m. to 2 p.m., 6 p.m. to 10 p.m.

It follows, therefore, that the normal day strength at any given time was only half of that at night, i.e., one sergeant and four to five constables, while at night there were two sergeants and from eight to ten constables. It was one of the nightly sights to see the night duty section emerge from the Police Station (equipped with their smoky oil lamps) and parade up St. Peter's Street in Indian file on the kerb edge, 'peeling off' at their respective beats.

The last man – or 'tail-end Charlie' – carried a stout walking stick to indicate he was on boundary beat. This beat took him around the lanes and footpaths to Merton and Nackington Farms, the Gate inn, Barton and Hoath Farms, on to the Polo Ground and Sanatorium. To prove that he had reached the extremity of his beat, the constable would note and, if necessary, report upon the number and names of patients. This information was recorded on a notice at the entrance to the sanatorium.

During the night, hot coffee was prepared by the reserve man at the police station and each man was allowed 15 minutes for his refreshment. It was during these short breaks that I was later to learn much of the history of the force and background of individuals, to say nothing of 'tricks of the trade.'

All beats were worked on a fixed route bases, points were made every 15 minutes and there was no discretion as to timing or route. If a constable was late, or missed a point, he had much explaining to do! Beats were worked so regularly, in fact, that by day, children on their way to school and housewives about their domestic work fixed their time by the passing of the constable.

No doubt less worthy individuals timed their activities in a like manner! Was it not that arch-criminal,

Charlie Peace, who said that his greatest and most feared enemies were noisy dogs and lazy policemen!

The only fixed point in Canterbury in 1914 was at the junction of High Street and St. Margaret's Street, several yards below the point now controlled by police. Both St. Margaret's Street and Mercury Lane were, of course, open to two-way traffic and if there were any reversing to be done the 'new-fangled' motor car gave way to horse-drawn traffic.

A junior constable was not trusted on this point until he had served for several years. Even then the older constables regarded a young man so honoured as something of an upstart! The normal tour there was four hours, except when relieved by the visiting sergeant for five to ten minutes.

Ports of Call

There were several 'ports of call' where traders and others well disposed towards 'their police' would readily provide a cup of tea. The 'High Street Man' was especially well provided for, since there were Mr and Mrs Britton, of Burgate – good friends to police! Messrs Abrahams (now Singers,) Mr Fortescue West, where the maids were always good for a cup of tea in early mornings often a cup of tea with a homemade cake during the afternoons.

Another early morning call was made at the bakery of Mr Jim Fayter in Burgate Lane - I recently had the pleasure of a chat with him in Canterbury. Other regular havens were provided by Mr and Mrs Skelton, at the Gun Restaurant, St. Dunstan's, and the nurses at the Kent and Canterbury Hospital in Longport, etc. These and several others went out of their way to show their regard and consideration for the man on the beat.

Hospitality of another kind was available at each and every one of the four breweries then operating in the city: George Boar's (Broad Street,) Ash's (Watling Street,) Flint's (St. Dunstan's Street) and Russell's (Sturry Road.) There were, of course, several legends concerning night duty constables and these establishments. One man, whatever his beat, made it a point of honour to visit each and every one of the breweries during each tour of duty. The story was told of another whose helmet was seen floating across a vat of fermenting beer like a ship in distress!

Extraneous Duties

The most important of such duty was that of fireman. The main body of the Force lived in the St. Peter's and St. Dunstan's area. Selected men formed the Police Fire Brigade and their houses were fitted with fire bells which, upon an alarm, were rung down by the duty officer. He also was responsible for calling the members of the two other brigades in the city, i.e., the Kent Brigade and the County Brigade, both of which were supported by local fire insurance offices.

It was sometimes suggested by the volunteer members of these brigades – perhaps not entirely without truth – that there was some delay between the calling of police personnel and the 'ringing down' of their own bells. The equipment of the fire brigade was of a most elementary nature, a truck (hand-propelled) containing lengths of hose, branches, stand-pipes and keys.

For water pressure, they depended upon the mains. There was sometimes a struggle between two contenders for a High Street hydrant where the pressure was far greater than in the side street. The most unpopular piece of fire equipment was the heavy escape which was housed under the Westgate Tower. To get that apparatus up Nunnery Fields required both tremendous strength and determination! Another set of fire ladders was kept in the Shambles (Longmarket) and the night duty man on Burgate beat was responsible for their readiness.

Other duties were visiting the Beaney Institute twice nightly – a relic of suffragette days; turning off main street lamps and switching on side lamps; closing and locking public lavatories; locking recreation ground; testing water pressure in mains; and early morning calls to police and other workers.

Customers! Both Friends and Enemies

Even at this time to mention names might give pain. There were, however, two men who, in their respective spheres, were both friends and enemies.

One was a poacher, Joe Gregory. His knowledge of the wild – and policemen's beats – was uncanny! It was extremely difficult to catch him and still harder to make a case 'stick' at court, for his knowledge of the Game Laws would have been a credit to a barrister!

The other was 'Matty' Hughes, who, when in full spate was quite a handful yet, when cold sober, he was quite a friendly man. His appearances at court were well over the century mark! He was quite honest and it was a complete waste of time sending an escort with him on the occasions when he became a guest at H.M. Prison. If given the warrant, he would certainly have presented himself at the gate! He was my first arrest in 1919 – his 63rd!

If the foregoing is of as much interest to older readers as it has been to me in recalling days gone by, I am more than satisfied. I further welcome the opportunity of making some contribution to the *Kentish Gazette* whose late editor, Mr G.R. Hews, gave me so much encouragement as a young policeman. It was he who advised me to learn shorthand and, in doing so, 'marked me down' for early promotion. – **R.C.M.J.**

Author's Note

It was in October 2009 that I first saw the oil painting of Robert Cyril Morton Jenkins in the executive corridor at Devon & Cornwall Police headquarters in Exeter. It was a few years however before I became curious about the subject of the painting – a seemingly tall man (although in reality a modest 5'10") with a military bearing and piercing eyes, one hand perched on the right hip, looking off into the distance. In 2012, I learned that the piece was painted in 1939 by Irish artist Stanhope A. Forbes, a resident of Newlyn near Penzance in the 1930s. A small plaque situated beneath the painting told me who he was and that he retired as Deputy Chief Constable of Kent.

It was a chance enquiry with the Kent Police Museum, then situated at Chatham Docks, that put me in touch with Robert D. Mott, a retired police superintendent and R.C.M. Jenkins' great-nephew. Throughout the course of 2013, I worked with Robert to create a profile of Jenkins which eventually ended up online. A year later I revisited the subject matter and wrote the online article 'R.C.M. Jenkins: A Gentleman at War' for the Devon & Cornwall Police Museum website. It received little coverage, and it was the original Wikipedia profile that caught the attention of Cyril's direct descendants Brian and Paul Jenkins, grandson and great-grandson respectively. On 18th March

2015, Paul contacted me on Twitter and enquired about my curiosity about his great-grandfather, and from that point forward the story of Robert Cyril Morton Jenkins unfolded.

It was a painful truth for Cyril that he would never know the identity of his biological father. Born on 16th May 1898 in Chelsea, he was registered as Robert Cyril Morton *Flint*. The field on the birth certificate that would record the name of the father was left blank. His mother, Isabella, was a nurse at the Chelsea Hospital and for reasons lost to time, she gave Cyril up for adoption. It seemed right given the ready availability of digital ancestry records to pay closer attention to this critical life event, and when I began to struggle I enlisted the help of Jill Drysdale, a genealogist based in Totnes, Devon. Jill's research provided tentative hints to a Scottish connection, suggesting at least that the maternal line originated outside Kent. The wider paternal mystery will likely never be solved.

The adoption left him however with no disadvantage; his adoptive parents were good people and gave Cyril a strong start in life. The image on the following page is the only known photograph of William and Bertha Jenkins.

William and Bertha Jenkins, centre, c1919. Ethel Jordan, the future Mrs Cyril Jenkins, is stood on the far left. *(Brian P. Jenkins)*

Acknowledgements

My sincerest gratitude is reserved for Brian P. Jenkins, who gave me his personal blessing to write the story of his grandfather's life. Brian provided photographs, anecdotes and a written contribution without which I am certain would have made this book many pages shorter. Furthermore, Brian gave his spare time to check my work for errors, and the final work is all the better for it. I am thankful that Brian's nephew Paul put me in touch with Brian in 2015.

Peter Jenkins likewise provided anecdotes and photographs, greatly expanding my knowledge of his father, Donald Jenkins, and of how the Forbes painting passed from the Jenkins family into the ownership of Devon & Cornwall Police.

Robert D. Mott has been a constant source of encouragement over the years and likewise gave his spare time to check my work and transcribe the *Kentish Gazette* article and provide insight into Kentish life, lore and locations. It was a pleasure to finally meet Robert and his wife Heather in Canterbury in 2015 after much long-distance correspondence.

Anna Derham, former curator of the Kent Police Museum, provided information and encouragement early on, as did her successor Holly Wells.

Carmen Talbot listened to me in the first place and allowed me to tell the story in its early form in the online domain. I am grateful to Carmen and the volunteers of the South West Police Heritage Trust that the Forbes painting was restored, rehung and relocated to a safer place with the help of a grant from the Heritage Lottery Fund.

Genealogist Jill Drysdale gave her spare time to investigate Cyril's origins and answered many unknowns.

Kristina L. Evans applied her artistic skills to help me design the covers and other aesthetic aspects of the book.

Roger Hext, Reverend Alan Pinnegar, Ken Searle, Brian Edmunds, Angela Sutton-Vane, Katie Herbert, Hilary Bracegirdle, Roy Ingleton, Simon Dell and Mr Roberts of Truro all gave their support in various forms.

Finally, I am grateful for the kind assistance of all of the Kent County NARPO members who got in touch and provided their reflections.

About the Author

Mark Rothwell is an author and police historian based in Somerset, south-west England. He was born in Liverpool in 1986 and relocated to the West Country in the year 2000. In January 2017, he published his first book 'Policing the West Country: 180 Years of Policing in Devon and Cornwall.'

Email: mrothwell643@hotmail.co.uk
Twitter @TheRothOfKhan

References

[i] The History of the 11th (Lewisham) Royal West Kent Regiment by Captain R.O. Russell M.C., p.132-133
[ii] The History of the 11th (Lewisham) Royal West Kent Regiment by Captain R.O. Russell M.C., p.150-151
[iii] *The Cornishman* 15 February 1940
[iv] "Penzance Police Court" *The Cornishman* 27 June 1940
[v] History of Policing of the Isles of Scilly, by Professor Wyn Grant
[vi] "Penzance Tribute" *Western Morning News* 12 November 1941
[vii] *Police Review* 16 January 1943
[viii] "Ramsgate Has More Policemen" *Thanet Advertiser* 4 April 1950, p.4, col.1

Printed in Great Britain
by Amazon